AIN' N⊘BODY TOLD ME IT WAS ABUSE

JUANITA FRASIER

Kingdom Builders Publications LLC

Unless otherwise noted, all Scripture references are from the King James Version of the Bible, public domain. All rights reserved.

ISBN
978-0-578-35576-4

LCCN
2022900835
Printed in the USA

Author
Juanita Frasier

Editor
Lakisha S. Forrester

Publisher
Kingdom Builders Publications, LLC

Cover Design
LoMar Designs

Cover Picture
ID 114253740 © Rawpixelimages | Dreamstime.com

DEDICATION

For every parent, child, partner, spouse, friend, boss, and leader who abused or who was abused, read my story. Feel my pain. Recognize the healing. Touch and feel the HOPE. Do the work. Change. You can. I did.

PROLOGUE

I remember being a bouncy, bubbly little girl with a great sense of style and a sincere attitude for sharing and giving. I wanted to be loved and connected to people in a way that showed I cared about their hearts and the smiles on their faces.

At five years old, I discovered that I was different. Music came flying from my fingers. I was so young and could sing and play the piano without training. When I became aware and acquainted with my singing voice, I liked it and noticed others liked it too. I was considered to be a child prodigy.

Outside of our own local assembly at Saint Mark Holiness Church, Mama would take me around to afternoon singing programs, church conventions, and other functions she was a part of so I could experience the culture of church music. There were ensembles, trios, duets, choirs, quartets, and soloists. Mama was also a choirman and liked singing too.

When asked to be on any program to play the piano and sing, I would nervously give away my matching jeweled necklaces, bracelets, and ring ensembles to other children my age and older in an attempt to apologize for being a good musician and singer. My real motive was to appease kids who were on the program with me so they wouldn't be mad at me for my God-given talent. I just wanted to be accepted, loved, and remembered.

When Mama discovered I was giving away the things she bought me, she scolded me and switched it up to buying candy necklaces. I ate a few of my tasty jewelry, but I would still share and give them away. I loved the way the kids would be surprised or happy, and that made me feel good. I thought I was changing their lives, so I didn't care much about the beatings because I knew the pain would wear off after a while.

* * *

When I began kindergarten, I could hardly wait to go to school daily in a long two-toned station wagon that I loved. It was a great time because I didn't have to be in a big old car alone. My classmates rode in it too. I've always hated the separation and isolation I felt when riding in the back seat of my parents' car. If I couldn't sit next to my mama or daddy, then please let there be someone to sit with me in their large hearse-style back seat. I loved company, teamwork, and togetherness. I guess that stemmed from me being an only child at home.

My classmates and I all sounded the same with our giggles and little talking voices riding in the back of the vehicle. I loved all my classmates. We always saw eye to eye because we were all at eye level. Such great times.

I distinctly remember the breakfast smell of grits with a spat of yellow butter and cut pieces of link sausages most mornings. I could hardly wait to get there to enjoy those great staples presented in a light turquoise bowl with a small glass of milk. The scent filled the air. Breakfast was amazing, but the main reason I loved school was because of my teacher, Miss Salley Mae. She always smelled very pretty and her thick long curly dark tresses were so beautiful.

Miss Salley Mae wore glasses like Mama, but she was nothing like her. She smiled a lot and was very kind. She loved all of her students, and I was one of them. Miss Salley Mae loved me. In my mind, I was her child and she was my school mommy.

I loved circle time on our large colorful square carpet on the shiny wooden floor in our school. She would let us sit next to her and on a few occasions, a child could sit on her lap to turn the pages of a nursery book she'd read to us. I was one of those children. I wasn't the squirmy child. I was the touchy-feely and sniffing child.

When I sat on her lap, it had nothing to do with turning pages. I just wanted the touch; the bond. I touched her hair, smelled her clothes, and rubbed her face. Her hair was soft and bouncy, and when I touched her deep brown face, it felt so smooth.

She would group us for lunch and crafts. Although I had a great imagination, I couldn't draw, do cutouts, or make things with my hands. I was horrible at crafts, but my hands were really good at playing little songs on the piano, even though I couldn't prove it because Miss Salley Mae did not have a piano at school. I was also good with song time on the carpet. I loved singing the nursey songs and some of my Sunday school songs.

* * *

I remember the weekend Mama brought home some clothing for my daddy, herself, and me. I didn't understand the hand-me-down concept. I thought clothes only came from the store and in a bag with a tag and receipt. But when she brought clothes home in a box or a grocery bag, it was still like Christmas time, going through the things and finding something I liked and could wear. Mama got these items from her buckers'[1] house upon clearing clothes from her children's closet.

The only pieces of clothing I found in the big box that I ever loved

---

[1] White folks

were a pair of white cowgirl boots and a white flair-tailed, hand-sewn pearl skirt. It was intriguing because one would normally wear pearls on a string around the neck, on the wrist, or as a ring. That skirt was the most beautiful thing I had ever seen. I felt like a very rich cowgirl in a parade. It was pretty enough to wear to church, so it was a no brainer that I would wear my new clothes to kindergarten.

Monday morning, we all got out the vehicle headed into our place of great adventure in kindergarten. Everyone loved my skirt. I saw how it made my friends feel and how it made me popular, so I would pull off a pearl so my classmates could be happy, be my friend, and not forget the feeling. By the time it was recess, I had given away more than half of my pearls to my friends and the boys (because they deserved to feel good too). Besides, everyone likes gifts, right?

Miss Salley Mae noticed pearl beads all over her floor. She called me just before going out to play.

"What have you done? What happened to your beautiful skirt?"

"Nothing. I gave some of the pearls to my friends. They love them."

In a gentle voice, Miss Salley Mae asked, "Why did you do that? It is such a pretty skirt. Well, it's not pretty anymore because you've taken practically all the pearls off. What is your mother going to say? You should not have done that. I've got to call her."

"Oh, she won't mind. She didn't even buy it for me. She got it from her buckers' house. My mama's buckers are rich."

Boy, was I wrong! I didn't entirely learn the double-edge truth about love, feelings, giving, ownership, or anger and sadness. First off, I never got to wear the skirt again because I ruined it by giving the prettiest part away. At the time, it seemed appropriate. Secondly, I learned things don't last forever, and I eventually outgrew my beautiful white cowgirl boots. And thirdly, yes, I got a good tanning[2] for being so free.

Was it worth it? Yes, for that moment. Besides, the church says, "It's more blessed to give than receive." But I guess I had to know how to decipher there were different rules for children who had a heart to give. To say the least, my mama and I were disappointed that I destroyed my cowgirl skirt, but ain' nobody ever told me that children don't have the power or privilege to give their things away and all their things still belong to their parents.

* * *

First grade was a big school and presented all brand new things. New writing paper, writing composition books, notebooks, yellow No. 2 pencils, construction paper, new reading books...and they were all delightful.

My teacher, Miss Adams, passed out some construction paper, scissors, and a bright yellow box of Crayola crayons. There were eight bright pencil shaped colors. Before that day, I had never seen anything quite like that. That was my first encounter with sticks of crayons that weren't big, uncovered, and uneven (made perfect for a kindergartener's hands).

The colors in the box from left to right were: black, blue, brown, green, violet, orange, red, and yellow. The color that called my name was the Violet color, which was in the center of the box.

The colors were so bold and fresh that before I colored with them, I

---

[2] A beating; a whipping

inspired to try one of them. The Purple one. As I peeled away its wrapping, with great anticipation, my mouth was expecting a bold rich flavor. When I bit down with the hopes of a grape flavor from the right side of my mouth where all the good flavor is experienced, I got the shock to my taste buds and the shock of my life. It had absolutely NO TASTE. In fact, it tasted like a candle…and how would I know that comparison? You guessed it! I tried a red candle before. I couldn't read, so I didn't know it didn't have two functionalities. I learned my first school lesson that day. Those beautifully wrapped colors in that beautiful shiny box were not made to be ingested. I spat that crunchy and tasteless wax out of my mouth with the fierceness. I then looked around to see if anyone saw my experience. No one did except Joseph (who seemed to always have his eyes on me waiting to be a tattletale), who in that instant said nothing, and just gave me a smirky smile.

I didn't turn against Crayola crayons that day because I tried my hand at a new discovery that wasn't supposed to be so. I discovered that colors are for making paper pretty on the outside, and that would be your good feeling on the inside. I had planned to ask Mama to buy me a box immediately.

* * *

I've loved that color for as long as I can remember. My mama would usually buy many colored foods, drinks, treats, fruits, and vegetables that tasted so amazing. Some with no smell, yet others with bold aromas. My favorite ones were the purple ones: blueberries, grapes, eggplants, beets, onions, cookies, candies, lollipops, frozen icicles, hard and soft candy (wrapped and unwrapped), grape Kool-Aid, and grape breakfast juice. I'd get the giggles every time I was in proximity of purple. The taste, the smell, and the look had me enchanted.

* * *

I remember one of my mama's cousins would visit us frequently. I referred to her as 'Aunt Millie.' I loved her hugs. She always called me 'Princess' and she often brought me gifts. I loved sitting on her lap because it was very wide and cushiony. She was a thick, sweet, and nice lady who was like a human grape lollipop. When I'd sit in her lap, I would make the opportunity to get coddled, and my takeaway was smelling and touching her face. Her face would usually smell good. I loved gently scratching her high round cheeks and putting my tongue on one of them, expecting to get a taste of grape since her exceptionally dark skin was that color. Her skin had a slight purple tint to it. I can't forget the day she asked me, "Why you scratching and licking me?"

"I'm just waiting for your cheeks to pop. Your cheeks look like grapes."

She laughed, tickled me, gave me a great big kiss, and dismissed me from her lap.

CONTENTS

THE COOKIES IN THE COOKIE JAR

When you are a child, you only have the authority to eat, play, and sleep. As a Baby Boomer, growing up in the south in the 50s, you did what you were told (if you were not rebellious). In my first opinion of things, my surrogate mother had me bound and gagged in my mind. But as a child, I didn't entirely know that.

I've never been in the military, but the technique used to build a soldier or a marine is to strip them down to the bare minimum in character, confidence, and scruples. This is done mostly by drill sergeants who insult, manipulate, and degrade, pushing the candidates beyond the brink so everyone, including the candidates, will know what they are made of. Are they military material? They have to be willing to fight for what they can have or take a flight, never realizing what is capable or possible.

I remember the day my mama told me about the cookies in the cookie jar. I didn't know at that time she was breaking me, manipulating me, and degrading me, while in her estimation, training me with her strong drill instructor tactics.

Let me interject for all parents. We do have the power over our young children to steer them in any direction, hopefully in moral and right ones.

The Holy Bible isn't a book of suggestions, rather a book of instruction and training. **Proverbs 22:6** is clear in the message that we "train up a child in the way he should go: and when he is old, he will not depart" from the principles of that training. The Scriptures also speak to the responsibility of parents on integrity and character. There are parents who go too far with insults, discipline, discouragement, and punishment. **Ephesians 6:4** and **Colossians 3:21** both remind fathers [parents] not to provoke their children to wrath [anger], lest they be discouraged, but to "bring them up in the nurture and admonition of the Lord."

Then there are some parents who give entitlement to their children, allowing them to make their own decisions at a very young age and get whatever they want any time they want it.

Both of these styles can have lasting effects. One will teach them freedom to be more conscious about their role in decision making, where they are welcome to make mistakes and decisions for the art of greater decisions made down the road. This is effective learning.

The other shows how senior people say, "I've made this mistake, so learn from my mistake" or "Do what I say and not what I do." This could be looked at as one who can be steered from his own intelligence and make decisions to the betterment or detriment of someone else's choices.

Either parenting style can have rewards that will take them to new levels of success, which is favorable and desired, or have repercussions that can lead to a roller coaster ride of disaster, and no one will want to feel or deal with that.

* * *

Mama and I went to the market called Big Star Grocery. She ordered a large list of groceries as she commonly did every other week. We walked every aisle, picking up food, nonperishables, and some fun things for each of us (or let's just call them rewards for just being at the store). When we returned home, she turned the key off to the ignition switch on our beautiful red and white 1952 Chevy with the comfy white seats that I loved. She used the same key to open the trunk. There it was…a trunk full of neatly creased, brown paper bags filled with groceries. Mama and I made a path from the trunk to the front door stairs all the way through to the kitchen with the groceries. We walked a few good times before finally putting all the bags in the house. Once we were done, our final march to the vehicle was to close the trunk.

In that moment, I felt good about our 'Mother & Daughter' relationship. I felt I was fulfilling the Golden Rule learned in Sunday school: "Do unto others as you have them do unto you." I felt great because I sensed that she was liking me. I was feeling some kind of happy because I was sharing a moment with my beautiful mother. I wanted that feeling to go on forever. Most times, I was not so fortunate. I was careful to put away the sugar and rice sacks, the milk in the fridge, and the great number of canned goods in the cabinet. I also put away the washing powder and the bars of soap, while my mama focused on separating the meats, vegetables, and bagging them for the freezer. After her task was over, I waited for that special thing she would do with the snacks. Little Debbie Raisin Creme Pies, cheese balls, and coconut cookies were our usual goodies. The snacks were added to the daily lunch for the family. They were compartmentalized in certain jars and drawers, with the exception of the ice cream and the coconut cookies. The cookies, which were my absolute favorite, were always accessible in a heavy lead crystal cookie jar.

Some days when she was singing and cutting up the meat, I just knew I was going to get a Dixie paper cup full of cheese balls or a paper towel with two or three cookies, along with a Dixie paper cup filled with milk. Everything had to be perfect from my perspective. I needed to be sure everything would be in its place; no awkward movements; only smiles with just the right amount of questions or answers; and the best behavior with the finest niceties!

Things were going perfectly, when suddenly the worst fear happened. While humming one of her favorite church songs, my mama turned and looked at me as if she'd never seen me before and said, "Dees cookies I'm 'bout to put in dis here cookie jar has already been

14

counted. You can only git two cookies and if you git more than that, I'll know about it, and you'll be beaten with many stripes." You talk about scared of my mama. I was more scared of her than Jesus Christ. I only ate the cookies she gave me.

All kinds of thoughts started coming to my mind. *What if she forgot the count? What if one of the cookies broke in my favorite crystal cookie jar?* I was already getting my share of beatings a day. I was not trying to add anything other to my plight. I got a whippin' for being clumsy, talking to my imaginary friends, talking proper, walking grown, having emotions, rocking back and forth on my knees, drinking from the milk carton, watching TV well after lights out, looking in her direction when she's talking to an adult, asking too many questions, and not asking before going in the refrigerator for drinks or snacks. The list just kept on going. There were so many rules to keep up with. I call them fencing rules, which are rules made up as you go.

As a child, you just knew that you would get punished for breaking those ever-changing, unspoken rules. Now that I'm an adult, I see how we have the upper hand. There's no way one could instantly know these rules as a child. Usually, my education would come in a slap, knock, brush, shoe, extension cord, or from her iron fist.

Mama was very devout and as she put it, "I'mma upstanding Christian woman in this community and ain' nobody can spot my life." Living holy and set apart meant something to black folks born in the late 1800s through the early 1900s, possibly because they had nothing else of their own. Their lives had been snatched, stolen, and upstaged by white folks for centuries. They had to learn to bow down in order to live. Coloreds were not stupid. They saw how life worked, and they brought some of those ungodly practices into their own shanties, shacks, and better housing. For generations, demeaning and degrading mentality grew in our culture to keep one humble and alive.

My parents were both *saved, sanctified, and filled up with the Holy Ghost, on their way to heaven, and enjoying the trip.* This was a congregational saying in a lot of black churches. It was a catch-on phrase that helped the saints in their crazy lives. Yes, Mama would be loving on Jesus with everything within her and she taught me to love HIM too. But were we capable of loving ourselves?

I once heard a man say about his mother, "She's doing all she knows to do; she just doesn't know much." I've thought of the same phrase of my own mother. I think this could be a classic explanation of those raised in the dark age of slavery and degradation. My daddy was a gentler soul. He was not much on the rod of correction, but he did believe in discipline. He gave life nuggets, of which I am still using today. He learned how to love and to tolerate his wife's insecurities, meanness, and bossiness. At times, she was like a volcano waiting to erupt. On the flip side of my mama's rough side was a smooth-skinned, long black-haired, skinny-legged, wide-hipped, redbone descent of Cherokee Indian who loved nice things, nice clothes, and could cook you into a fit. Everybody loved her mouth-watering dishes. Lord, that woman could cook!

Behind closed doors, there was a distinct difference in how Mama acted when she was at home. She was more refined as an upstanding Christian at work and church. Sometimes I would often wonder if she was nicer when I wasn't in proximity to do something to mess it all up. My whole life I felt like I was always putting out 200% just to get 50% back from her. There is a Good Book quote I consider a rule. It says, "Cast thy bread upon the waters: for thou shalt find it after many days."[3] This simply means do good, and good will come back to you. That rule didn't always work for me with Mama.

In retrospect and in defense of my beautiful mother, I believed she loved me. When she saw me and chose me, she might have had high

---

[3] **Ephesians 11:1**

hopes for me. But we all can testify that things don't always work out in life as it is in your mind.

To Mama's credit, her love was more to show wealth and prominence. It was similar to when the head of the house would work and sacrifice so the woman could be at home. That's how love was shown. Mama shared in supporting the household. She made sure I looked my best with the finest clothes she and my daddy could buy, toys galore, electronics, and musical instruments. Anything that a child could want, I had it. That was so wonderful, especially when I got to share with cousins or an occasional visitor. I definitely had things – nice house, nice room, nice toys, beautiful clothes, and beautiful hairstyles – but I never had her. She was just not that touchy-feely mom shown on television; the one I needed in my soul and in my space.

On the one hand, I felt she was proud of me because I always looked nice when she dressed me, I sang and played the piano, I was crowned Miss Black Florence, and even though I had a learning challenge, I graduated high school on time, and had some college courses. On the other hand, I felt she was ashamed of me because I learned differently and because of the many illnesses I was diagnosed with. I believe Mama didn't want me to be a spectacle because she didn't want to be judged for choosing a sickly little girl.

There are so many stories about the spirit of my mama's demons. Clearly, her dysfunction turned us dysfunctional. Her first and only birth child, my brother (who is 28 years older than me) was a silent alcoholic. And I became a ball of nerves, nervous about everything, depressed, and suicidal.

The doctors diagnosed me as a manic-depressive, which is the modern-day name for bipolar disorder. Mama always contended that she was NOT the crazy one; I was. She said I was crazy because I had epileptic seizures. She referred to the convulsions as "fits." I also suffered greatly with migraine headaches and asthma. I had migraine headaches early in childhood. I've been stricken for 15 days at a time. No rest, no anything, just throbbing and stabbing pains in the head. I used to think if I could cut off my head and put it under the mattress and mash it, the pain would go away. Of course, I never tried it. I just couldn't take noise. It was too loud to whisper, the beat of my pulse was loud, and the thump of the headache was so loud; it continued giving me a headache. I couldn't take the sun, lamp, or ceiling light, walking, chewing, or anything physical. I was usually in bed, but I could tolerate music under my pillow with an extremely low volume, trying to be soothed by the music so the pain would go away. Pills didn't usually work, so Mama would take me to the doctor for a shot. The shots didn't help the migraines go away; they just silenced them for a small span of time and every other feeling in my body. I'd sleep up to four days.

The pain of the headaches was just as bad or worse as the three types of seizures (petit mal, grand mal, and Jacksonian) I lived with. The doctors told my parents I was not normal and needed shock treatments. At twelve years old, Mama took me multiple times a month for almost a year. Even though I had epileptic seizures, the clinicians would induce the "fits" to make me better. *What? That's an oxymoron.* To justify their science, I had to go to the room where the gurney was located. They hooked my head up to the strangest apparatus, put lead in my mouth, straps at my feet, legs, and chest, and flipped me upside-down for the 15-minute, plugged up shock treatments, so I wouldn't choke from the foaming saliva from my mouth.

The treatments were some of the most horrid experiences of my childhood, just so I could be called normal. Alongside all the shock treatments, I had to take that nasty medicine called Ritalin syrup, coupled with Dilantin, Phenobarbital, and Sinequan. I was a straight up medicinal zombie.

All that for normalcy? It's a wonder that I have any live cells in my brain, or cognitive skills to think and put things together. I recall crying and telling my daddy I didn't want to go through the shock treatments anymore. He wiped my tears and said to me in his tenderest voice, "You know what nomial is? It's the setting on a washing machine. Nomial is where you are and what you do at the moment. Everybody's got dey own kinda nomial." That made me feel so amazing. Not too many months after his encouragement, a law was passed to ban shock treatments in children under 18.

By my next birthday, I didn't have to deal with the anguish, fear, and inhumane treatment that went along with shock treatments for my seizures and vascular pain. They tried something new called chiropractic treatments. It was much more humane, and it actually felt good. I don't know if it cured or even helped me, but I didn't have to have a lot of spinal taps or crazy experimental happenings as much. What a phenomenal birthday present for me!

Now with asthma, my inability to breathe was so intense. There were days while trying to breathe in and out from a tight chest, I would lay down because of exhaustion from trying to gasp for air. When I tried to inhale or exhale, the bed would literally shake and move. Mama's love was genuine, though to some, it seemed warped. She didn't want me to suffer, so she would try little home remedies.

I'm going to warn you in advance that what I'm about to share is graphic, uncensored, and may make you barf, but it is what I experienced. There were days when breathing was such a chore. My mama would draw a bath of cool water and use a washcloth to pour it over my body, then rub my chest down with Vicks VapoRub and put me to bed under a heap of blankets to help me sweat the asthma out. But this night was different. While I soaked, Mama left my side to get a bathroom-style Dixie cup. She gave the cup to me and had me to excrete in it, then told me to drink that warm urine. Warm drinks were usually inviting, like the good feeling when you drink

19

warm milk or hot tea. However, after that sip, I looked at my mama in shock.

The color was similar to the color of a Mountain Dew soda, so I wasn't expecting the bitter, foul, disgusting taste. It was nasty! She said, "Drink it! Drink it all down. It'll cut dat asthma. You don't want dat asthma, do you?" I shook my head hard and fast while trying to ingest it with a despicable look on my face and the unpleasant taste going down my throat.

From a child's perspective, I was thinking, "It came from me, so how could it NOT be good for me, right? Besides, my mama loves me and wants me well, so this could work out." I felt some kind of way, but the compassion in her eyes made me trust her decision. Neither one of us liked the onslaught and effects of asthma. I believe she thought she was helping. But ain' nobody told her it was abuse.

At the direction of an old preacher, Mama, by the grace of God, used healing olive oil to coat my flesh after casting the devil out of me with fire. She first opened a clothes hanger and put it on top of the stove. When it was red hot on the ends, she pricked me all over my skin. I squirmed between her legs because of the heat. Mama demanded I take it because it was going to help me. She prayed, "Come out in the name of Jesus, you foul devil!" The experience seemed awful for us both. Nonetheless, her maternal desire to have me be well took her to great measures outside the normal limits. Mama took the olive oil and prayed, "Heal my child, Lowd, heal my child." She rubbed me ever so tenderly, helped me with my pajamas, and I went to bed thinking I was going to be cured from all my illnesses. She believed. So I believed. Because she did it all in the name of Jesus, I didn't know it was wrong because ain' nobody told me it was abuse.

I had old parents and they "chose" me to be their child. According to Mama, I was sickly, ugly, and nobody wanted me. She often said I was nothing and my mama before me was nothing. WOW! To me, that was a completely off the wall remark. I tried to put it all together in my head what she was saying. "But aren't you my mother?" I asked inside. Before 12 years of age, I didn't know what those statements meant, yet I heard it multiple times a week.

THE CRUELTY OF ADOPTION

Being adopted for me was a sense of belonging to nothing or no one. Being given over to another family is being stripped from your own inheritance. Being received by another family is an interruption of what you were and an intrusion of what the surrogate family is familiar with. Adoption is blending out while the folk around you act as if you're blending in.

The stigma of adoption was so obvious that years later when my sons became adults, they revealed to me they felt the same homelessness and helplessness I felt. I was more adaptive in receiving what was dealt to me because I just needed a place to belong. However, to them, they had no real family of cousins, aunts, uncles, or grandparents. Their dad's family was not a close-knit family, yet they all belonged to each other. The family I grew up with was very close-knit, however, there was that empty feeling of being an outsider or a stranger, somewhat of a sojourner. My children were the image of their parents who they knew existed. I was the image of somebody, but I didn't have a clue of who that somebody was. I was existing as an imposter.

The Saturday morning my mama told me I was adopted was a day that I will never forget, but wish I could never remember. I was 11 years old. I was crushed, devastated, and confused. She said so many negative things over time, but the words that seared me the most on that day was that no one wanted me and I was going to wind up an orphan, but she came along and "rescued" me, so I should be thankful. If it weren't for her, I wouldn't be here or anywhere, she told me. This was the day I succumbed to my emotions and DIED. I belonged to nothing. I didn't think she loved or liked me, my teachers didn't seem to like me, my peers didn't seem to like me, nor did my mama's birth son and his wife seem to like me. I was almost convinced not to like me…so nothing mattered. I tuned all the bad feelings out of my mind and walked around numb just to survive. My soul was so bruised and battered, year after year, from verbal, emotional, and physical cruelty. I had to eventually divorce my mama's negativity from my ears, heart, and soul, so I would not dry up from emotional poison and ill nourishment.

The one person who consistently advocated for me and stood up for me was a godly man who loved me with all his might. But his love, my mama thought, was a cloak for me, and she didn't like it one bit. She hated my relationship with most people and said things like, "Stop being so happy. You just too happy."

Here comes another one of those fencing rules. "I want you to stop kissing your daddy goodnight." That's right! She forbade me to say I love you to him, hug, or kiss him goodnight, or show any type of affection. When she said to me, "I want you to stop kissing and licking up on your daddy. That don't look good," I was in the first grade. I was very inquisitive until my curiosities were dulled by…you guessed it…Mama. I asked my mama why did I have to stop saying I love you to my daddy. To me, my daddy and my mama were both the same because they were my parents.

Unfortunately, she didn't have the answer that I could appreciate. She simply said, "Did you hear what I said? It don't look good. Don't tell a man you love him. He'll do what he wants to do to you. I bet not ever hear talk of you saying that or doing that. You hear me?" I had to say, "Yes, ma'am," but without understanding. My daddy, in his wisdom, uttered not a word, but the love we shared as parent and daughter was ever-present, though unspoken. I trusted my daddy, so I went with the rule.

One would have to surmise that Mama saw more than she would ever say. She had sisters younger than she was and older as well. She also had many brothers. Maybe prior to marriage to my daddy, someone did something to her or to someone she really loved. A really mean and cruel thing, I imagine. As I got much, much older, I could then understand the minds of deviant people. The ones who tell you what you want to hear in order to get what they would probably never get without their coercions. I felt the lessons were for later, for boys or men who would try to get in my ear and my private parts...but not my DADDY! He's my DADDY!

Another horrible quote of Mama's was, "I can tell you is man struck." I was 9 or 10 years old and just started grade school. *What could that possibly mean?* It didn't feel like it was a compliment. It was like a hate gene took over Mama's thoughts and soul.

Maybe she was thinking, 'She's not our child, so she could have a sex-crazed gene from her mama who had three children prior to her," or "Maybe this child could work her magic on my husband."

This was my daddy! This only proves that hurting people hurt people and wrong information will mess it up for everyone. Ain' nobody told my mama saying things like that was abuse.

One day my daddy became gravely ill. The ambulance had come to carry him to the hospital. We lived several blocks from the downtown infirmary. When I heard about him, adrenalin took over and I ran as fast as my feet would move all the way to the hospital. I was out of breath, but when they let me in to see him, there he was in a hospital bed. I saw him very differently, very vulnerable. For as long as I could remember, he never had a hospital visit. I was so scared that he was going to die. My mama and some nurses were in the room. The nurses were tending to him. I took courage and said to him, in a panicked and loud voice, "Daddy, I love you. Don't die, Daddy. I will never stop saying I love you. I don't care who tells me to stop. I will never stop saying I love you. I love you. I love you. I love you! You can't die, Daddy. I love you and I want you to live." Then I kissed him all over his head and hands. My emotions broke and I felt a release from my innermost being. It was insurmountable.

It was love! I was free, and his face lit up as if I was the most famous person that he had ever seen. He was free to say to me, "I love you too!"

* * *

The silent struggles and pain I carried (because you'd better not speak what goes on in the house) was soothed by going to church, which was so inspirational to me. I was impressed and lifted by the great rhythmic and joyful songs and melodies, hearing the emotional talks from the young and old Christians, and watching people, even my mama dance to the music. I loved it. When I was four or five, I would see my mama dance, shout, and cry. It reminded me of me when she would give me a spanking. I would cry, scream, and dance about. She was my mom giving me a beating; and God was her Father. I would cry and ask God to stop beating my mama so maybe she would stop beating me. I was just in my imagination. I didn't grasp the reality of things.

When I was four years of age, I distinctly remember banging on any flat surface as if it were a musical instrument. WHEN GOD GAVE ME MUSIC, it literally saved my life. I would sing every day, no matter where I was or whether I had a piano or not. The music was my salvation, and the gospel music was my blues. With emotional turmoil, confusion in my soul, and sickness in my body, I thought everybody was like this. I thought all mamas and daddies were nice, of God, and everything was normal because ain' nobody told me I was abused.

Time didn't wait for me. I was turning into a young lady and I didn't know about life outside the grocery store, school, church, and my parents' home. I was quite comfortable playing with my dolls and tea sets, writing songs, singing, playing the piano, or writing poetry. There wasn't much on television except a few black TV shows. My absolute favorite show was *Medical Center*. It aired Monday nights at 8 o'clock.

On one particular night, Mama sent me to bed early as a punishment because of something dumb I did. I was willing to take a beating in exchange to stay up for Dr. Joe Gannon, who was the handsomest, blue-eyed man I had ever seen. I couldn't miss the opportunity to see the show. I went to bed crying. I was silently hoping to hear something from the show, but that didn't happen. I believe my mama turned the volume on the TV down on purpose. I thought to myself, "I'll make up my own show, I will be famous for my show, and then I'll be able to watch *Medical Center* whenever I want to." I began to carve out a plot on which to write my screenplay. I was hooked on finishing it, so much so until I took my typewriter to school.

My peers were inquisitive about my work. Some of my classmates started reading a few of the pages I had written. They made positive comments and pressed me for more pages each day. The teacher got involved and she let it get in the hands of the principal and his secretary. They helped me to go further. They didn't stop until my story was aired as a part of the *Medical Center* series in the early 70s. Several people edited my script, but I was credited as one of the writers (number six on the credit roll after the show).

I was offered an opportunity for a college scholarship upon graduation to the University of Southern California, with a concentration in journalism and creative writing (a Bachelor of Arts degree). Of course, my family didn't understand my creative side. Mama gave me no support. She said I would never leave the city because I was too sickly with "fits." She thought nobody needed the responsibility of my care and that it was her burden. So I continued writing and singing to myself and the LORD. Everywhere I went, I would soothe myself with a song. The arts were my only friends because the arts were true. We completely understood each other.

26

I don't know if holding me back from the things I liked, such as sports (track and field), music, going to college, and creating on every medium was considered abuse. I believe she genuinely didn't want me to be exposed to strangers in another state on the west side of the United States. Nevertheless, it is always unusually cruel, in my opinion, to squash someone's dreams.

THE LESSON FROM THE SUNDAY MORNING NEWSPAPER

My daddy did whatever it took to take care of his family. He worked for the Seaboard Coast Line Railroad, later renamed Amtrak. Mama did domestic work, but was later upgraded as a nurse's aide with the Crippled Children's Home. When Daddy was laid off, he went to work at the Shipyard in Newport News, Virginia. He always had a mechanic job. He was a hard worker and had hard labor jobs. When his job reopened at the railroad, he was called back, and they allowed him to pick up the years he had already invested.

I was in the ninth grade and new to a predominately white school. The school itself was newly built. It had only one graduation class prior to me joining the freshmen class. The principal was a dark-skinned, friendly but firm man.

At orientation, we were given a handbook, among other things for success in the new school. Seniors had more privileges than any other class. I quickly made new friends in Chorus and Home Economics.

For Christmas that year, Daddy bought me a green and silver detachable left/right speaker eight-track player. I was in heaven. I had Andraé Crouch's, Doug Oldham's, Edwin Hawkins's, and Marvin Gaye's eight track cartridges. You couldn't tell me anything. The year before, I had gotten a dainty reel to reel recorder. My parents invested musical equipment galore in me.

When I got the eight-track player, Daddy was sure to tell me NOT to take it to school. He warned me if I did, he would take it and I would never get it again. That was the carrot[4] because he knew I

---

[4] A simultaneous reward and punishment

didn't want to be without the newest craze. That should have deterred me, but…it did not.

To impress any would-be friends, I hid the dual-sided player in my bookbag and pulled it out on the bus. I played Edwin Hawkins's "O Happy Day." We were all singing on the bus and I was briefly feeling the love. When I got to school, I didn't take the time to conceal it in my backpack before entering the corridor. The science teacher and I exchanged greetings. He noticed my hand and said very gently, "You are an underclassman, so be careful and don't get caught with that player." I was very polite, thanked him, and headed to put it in my locker. I exchanged a few classes, then it was time for lunch.

Freshmen could not have electronics in the mall[5] area. My favorite hangout was the auditorium because a piano was there. I took my player in there because I could play the piano, sing, and listen to my music. A few of my classmates followed me there after lunch for singing. Nick, one of the guys who drove to school, said he was going to get some real music from his car. He came back with Stevie Wonder and the Commodores. Well, the bell rang for our next period class, so my player was openly exposed as I hurried to class before being late. My teacher, Ms. Lindley, was a small-framed white lady, who seemed to be easy, like a pushover. As we entered, she was trying to settle the class for a new lesson in math.

Nick put in Stevie Wonder's music in my eight-track player. She told him to put that away. "This is not chorus," she stated. At this time, the principal was walking down the hall of our corridor. He heard the music and opened the door to make sure he was hearing what he thought he heard. He did not disturb the class at that time, but shortly thereafter, the intercom came on in Ms. Lindley's class. It was the principal. He asked whose music player he heard coming from the room. When I thought I was popular for a day, all the students in my class threw me under the bus. They called out my

---

[5] Hangout area

name very loudly. The principal, Mr. Booker, said, "Send her to the office and have her bring the tape player too." My classmates spoke out in a disorganized concert, "Oooh, I told you. You know you're an underclassman." I was left to face authority alone. I told Nick to come too because it was his music the principal heard, but he put it back on me by saying it was my player.

When I got to Mr. Booker's office, he asked me if I had read the handbook. I answered, "Yes." He gave me a tongue lashing on going against the guides of the handbook and the fact that it was being played during class time. That was a no-no. He said to me, "You're suspended. AND…I'm going to take this player. You can get it back after school. Now get back to class before the next bell rings."

I went back to class, not speaking to any of my peers due to embarrassment and anger. When I completed the last class of the day, I ran to the principal's office before I boarded the bus. Mr. Booker was in his office and I politely asked if I could get the eight-track player because I had to catch the bus. He gave me a confused look, saying, "Oh, you thought I was talking about today? No, I was talking about June 3rd; the end of school!"

"What?" I was in shock. I never anticipated that answer. "You can't do that. My daddy will kill me if I don't bring my tape machine home."

"Why is that, Miss Nita? So your handbook and your daddy told you not to bring your electronics to school and you did it anyway. Wow, you have a problem."

I pleaded with him to give me another chance. He refused. This was not a good moment for either of us. I had built-up anxiety and displaced anger. People seemed to either take advantage of me, bully me, or tell me what I will or will not do. Mr. Booker was the villain

30

that was in the wrong place at the wrong time.

In a fit of protest, which quickly turned to rage, I stood up across from him and welled up spittle, hocked, and flew saliva all over his face. He HAD to know I was serious. He got all of it. My silent frustration, my built-up anger, my 'I'm not going to take another person's bullying.' *Somebody has to know I need to have some power about my own life.*

When it happened, it was already too late. I couldn't suck it back in. We were both in disbelief. He paused, then sat down very slowly, not uttering one more word. I remained standing, watching him pull out a pink slip from the middle drawer of his desk. He let me know that the suspension was upgraded to an expulsion for the indecent occurrence that just happened. I spoke not a word of this. I really didn't know what any of it meant, but I felt it would blow over. I was greatly concerned that Mr. Booker took my player and I wasn't able to get it back for six months and Daddy's gonna expect me to play my music in the house. Daddy definitely loved seeing me enjoying my things and my life.

I was as clever as I could be about this horrible thing I had done. The next day, I went to school. I hung in the mall area until first period. Then I went to my favorite place, the auditorium, to play my troubles away. I got caught, so I had to clean graffiti from the walls of the school. I was scolded not to return.

I still didn't tell. I got up the next morning, rode the bus, but didn't get off at my school. I rode to another school and got off there. I thought I could blend in. That did not work out for me either. Teachers were asking who the girl on the playground of the school was. They knew I was displaced. The school I formerly attended was contacted and a bus driver came to transport me back there. Ain' nobody told me that suspension was three days, but expulsion was indefinite.

I knew I was in trouble, so when I got home, I balled up a sheet of paper and stuck it under the handle of our rotary phone. It was off the hook without looking like it was. My parents didn't really talk on the phone that much during the week, so I was in the clear, I thought.

I didn't read so well, but I knew what our emblem looked like and if a letter came, I would retrieve it and tear it up so my parents would never know. This would blow over in a few days.

That Saturday morning, I was playing the piano in the front room. Mama was at work and Daddy was in the den, nodding off on the couch with the TV on. The doorbell rang. I was closer, so I answered. *OH, MY GOD*, it was my principal standing on our porch. I knew he didn't know my parents and my parents didn't know him. *How does he know where I live?* I had to think fast in my panic. "Hey, Mr. Booker."

"Good Morning, I'd like to speak with your parents."

"Umm, my parents are not at home."

"No problem, I'll just wait for them."

"Oh no, sir, you can't do that because I'm not allowed to have company when my parents are not here."

"Oh yes, what am I thinking? You always listen and obey your parents, follow instructions…just a kind young girl. I'll just wait in my car until one of them returns." His facetious remark shamed me.

About that time, my daddy was pulling up the suspenders on his pants to his shoulders, getting a little tidy as he approached the door. He extended his hand to greet the tall man and said, "Fraiser's my name."

32

"Allen Booker is my name, and I am the principal of your daughter's school."

Daddy asked me to move back out the way so the principal could come in.

Mr. Booker did not sit. He told the whole story. I had a sinking feeling in my stomach. I didn't know what to do. I was fully exposed. I wanted to run. I wanted to hide. I wanted to die. My daddy was pretty irate. When he told Mama, she beat me and fussed. I could not escape the hurt, pain, and humiliation I felt.

The next day was Sunday. Daddy got me up early and asked me to get dressed. He wanted to take me someplace. When I got dressed, he took me to the supermarket and gave me 75 cents to get a Sunday newspaper. We had no conversation to or from the store. I was taken aback by his weird request. He never asked for a newspaper before and never would he purchase a newspaper. Did someone get married, die, or make a great accomplishment and he just wanted to see them?

When we got back home, he called me in the parlor. He handed me the paper and told me to read the first page. I started with the first story. I struggled through that miserably. I even made up words and phrases just to appear to be reading well. I didn't know what he was up to or what he was getting at, but I just wanted to impress him.

What he said next sent a chill down my spine and it humbled me. "Now dat's why I'm sending you to school, so you can learn to read and write. You see, I can't read or write. I had to quit school. My daddy died, so I had to take up the slack. I went as far as the second grade. I had to work and support my mama, my sisters, and brothers. I was the oldest, so the 'sponsibility fell on me. We didn't have a car for the longest time. I think I was in my late teens before my mama nem got a car. We had a mule for farmin', but we couldn't use it for travelin' 'cuz he was a work mule, so I worked and worked to get us

33

something to ride in. Now you don't have to work. Me and ya mama tryin' to give you a good life, but naw. Instead of you taking in your learning, you get put out the school. Read me something else."

As he talked calmly to me, I cried and cried. He was filled with hurt and disappointment. I was so hurt that I hurt my beautiful daddy. I didn't know if I could come back from this. *Would I ever be forgiven?* This was worse than getting a beating. The knocks to the flesh wear off, but Daddy went to the heart.

He did that repeatedly until it was time to go to church. I cried all through the church service. I even went to the altar for prayer and forgiveness and still cried every day.

I went before the Board of Education in 14 days to learn my fate about returning to school. My daddy, mama, and I dressed up as if we were going to church. This was one of the scariest days of my life. We stood in the midst of seven people. They all had folders and a solemn face. Out of the seven, two were black (my principal, Mr. Booker and a well-dressed woman who sat on the board). With mostly white people on a panel, TV taught me I would not have a good outcome.

The meeting began. Daddy spoke up for me, saying, "Every child should be in school and that she was disciplined and punished long enough." My mama was silent that day. Everyone else spoke about me. Mr. Booker said his peace. Then it was my turn. I bawled like a baby. I repented. I begged for forgiveness and another chance. We were sent out of the office so they could scare me further and have me return with the verdict as if we were in court.

When we were called back in, they gave me a heavy chastisement and pardon. I fell on my knees at Mr. Booker's shoes and repeatedly apologized to him for such a horrible thing and thanked him for another chance. I told him he would never have any trouble from

34

me, and I meant that until the day I die. He genuinely forgave me.
He gave me back the eight-track machine. I was so glad to see it. I
also regret seeing it because it reminded me how horrible I was, and
it was ALL my fault.

When we walked out the office, Daddy beckoned for the player.
"You don't think I'mma letchu have this machine, do you? I told
you if you took it to school, I was gonna take it and you would never
get it back."

From that day to the day I married, it remained in his closet. When I
married, he showed it to me, but gave me $40 for it.

Wow.

THE BITE

I have had practically every form of abuse in the many years I have lived. Some were self-inflicted, some caused by my own naïveté, and the rest out of others' control or manipulation. I realize many women have a story of sexual misconduct done against them. It is a hard thing to deal with. I may not have made it out if I had been one of those who were sodomized, raped, or such. I think I can say I have never experienced sexual abuse, whether at the hands of a stranger, relative, friend, church official, in the workforce, a deranged boyfriend, or husband. I don't know if this one story may qualify as sexual abuse, but here it goes. You may chuckle or you may fall on the ground laughing, but this is my story.

I was in senior high school. By now, you know I love the arts. I was sold out on singing, playing the piano, writing, and acting. Wherever these were, that's probably where you would find me. This particular day, I stayed over in the chorus room working out a song I had written for our gospel choir for the Christmas program. I had permission from the chorus teacher. It was lunchtime and she was taking her lunch. Well, for me, working on music in the music room was my lunch. I didn't need to chew food because I was filled with every interaction of what I was doing.

While putting some finishing touches to the song for Miss Dabney to hear, one of my school's most famous football stars came in the music room. I thought he was lost. I had never seen him in music before and didn't know about his stardom as a football player. He stopped me by asking, "Did my brother just leave? I was supposed to meet him here."

"Who is your brother? I'm the only one here until Miss Dabney gets back."

"Carlos."

"Oh, Carlos. I know him. He has a real good tenor voice," I said, watching as he seemed to be casing the place.

At the time, it appeared as if he didn't believe me because he kept looking around. Little did I know, he was checking out the fact that this underclassman was all alone in a deserted class on a lifeless corridor. I didn't know to be afraid because Carlos was a very nice young man. Carlos was my friend and I loved his name and his singing voice. If Carlos is nice, his brother must be too, right?

Carlos's brother was nicknamed Jon-Jon and on the field, he was named 'The Thunda.' He asked me to sing him a song. I obliged, but he wasn't interested in my kind of music, which was mostly Christian songs.

"You ain' know no other songs, church girl?"

That was a little awkward, so I stopped playing and singing and told him that Carlos left when the bell rang.

"If you look for him, he's probably in the mall area or the cafeteria. I'mma let you go to look for him and I'mma lock the door."

Jon-Jon was slightly taller than me, but scrawny and muscular. He said to me, "I know you want me."

"Want you for what?"

"Aw, don't play, church girl. You know you want summa dis."

When he got very close to me, he pinned me to the wall. Now you know I was super scared of my mama. I could practically see her in a vision. She told me to keep my dress down and my drawers up. I just happened to have on a dress that day. Truth is, I always wore dresses. He was trying to restrain and contain me while he tried to pull up my dress. I didn't know what he was doing, what he was going to do, or even what he was capable of doing, but I knew it didn't feel good or safe. Consequently, I abruptly gained the strength of ten superheroes. I was for dear life trying not to get beat up by this guy or have him pull down my clothes. While he was going under my dress, something told me to retaliate. I opened my mouth and like a crazed pit bull, I locked my teeth into his left shoulder. I bit him like my life depended on it, and it did. I didn't let go immediately, only when I didn't feel his strong hands under my dress. He yelled out, released me, looked at me, and said, "What the hell? You bit me!" He bled and I wiped my mouth from the smell of his sweat and the taste of his salt and blood.

"If you don't tell, I won't tell," I said, feeling vindicated.

He left the chorus room, fussing and cussing. I could imagine him trying to explain that bite. But in order for him to tell his story, he would have to tell mine. He would probably be dismissed from the football team for his misconduct. I was never contacted, so I surmised he never told. He never looked at me, spoke to me, or anything else after that day in the chorus room.

KILLING ME SOFTLY AND SNATCHING ME HARD

January 4th. I will never forget that date. It was the date of my first talent show in my new school. I was given so many nicknames: giraffe neck, church girl, preacher girl, stuck up, and talented with music and words. I asked my mama to come to the school to see me perform in the talent show. I had a reason for asking her to come. First of all, I was doing songs outside my usual genre. I am most known for singing and playing Gospel music. I got my musical schooling from all the great Gospel singers. At home, I practiced my usual songs, but for the talent show, I would be singing songs from Bill Withers, Aretha Franklin, and Roberta Flack. I loved all of those artists. I had studied them day and night. When Daddy and Mama would leave the house, I hurried right on in singing and learning these other genres.

My parents did not believe in music outside of Gospel music. Mama said, "We don't sing reels[6] round yere." But if I wanted to be popular with my schoolmates, I needed to know some folk, pop, R&B, and social music.

For the talent show, I had to have just the right outfit, the right hairstyle, and the right songs. I wanted so desperately to be accepted by my peers and teachers, doing something I loved so well.

For about three weeks, I hounded my mama to attend the talent show, just to ensure she would NOT be there. If she told me she would not come, I would be safe, home free, and I could sing without inhibitions.

The first time I asked her to come to the talent show, she said, "I'm not coming out to dah schoolhouse. I hear you sing 'round this yere

---

[6] Secular music

house. I hear you sing at church. Why is I gon take off from work jess to hear you sing? YOU KNOW GOD!"

Inside, I was secretly screaming with excitement, "She's not coming! She's not coming!"

I tried a second time to seal the deal. "Mama, I'm going to be singing in the talent show. Will you come?"

"I done told you I ain' taking off my job to come yere you sang. You always singing 'round dis house and at church. You know God. Let 'em Use You."

It's a sure thing. She said it twice. We good. She's not gonna come.

There's a saying my daddy used to say: "Three strikes you out in anybody's ball game." So, the Wednesday night before the talent show, I asked one last time, just for security. "Mama, I'm gonna be in the talent show tomorrow. Don't you want to hear me sing at my school?"

"Nita, now I ain' gon tell you again. I told you I got to work."

Well, I put on my acting skills. "You never support me. You NEVER support me. All the kids at my school, their moms and dads come to their performances. They are proud of their children. You MUST be ashamed of me. Is that what it is, Mama? You're shame of me? I'll bet the lady you work for would go to her daughter's performance if she had one and she was asked. It starts at 10 in the morning."

I went all the way in. Bells and whistles and choirs and choruses. I worked her up in the guilt to my own detriment.

The next morning, I shampooed my hair and patted it down with a towel for the perfect round afro. I put on the gown Mama bought me for the Miss Black Florence Competition, except for the talent show, I wore it without the jacket, which made it a halter gown. SHOCKING! I wanted the curtain to open while I was seated on the piano stool. I didn't want to walk out to the piano. It would not be dramatic enough.

I heard the audience's stupefied comments about my hair and my long gown with the back out, but they were ready, anticipating the music, my music, my voice, though they had no idea the songs that would come out of my soul and my mouth.

I started off with, "Ain't No Sunshine When He's Gone." The auditorium went up. They were screaming and shouting my name. This was different for everyone who knew me. I did a medley of three songs. Usually when I sing, I close my eyes. I can imagine it and feel the music better. The next song was "Bridge Over Troubled Water." When I got to my final song in the medley, "Killing Me Softly with His Song," my eyes were still closed, so I didn't see the force to be reckoned with, but I felt a slight breeze. Then something gripped my wrist and as I opened my eyes, I saw...WHAT? It was Mama! I was still seated when she completely snatched me from the piano stool, wrecking my show; my performance.

THE WHOLE STUDENT BODY, including teachers and custodians, laughed at me. She snatched me down the stairs of the stage, saying, "Know you ain' out here singing no reels. You begged me to take off my job and come hear you do this mess!"

With her pocketbook in the other hand, she took it and beat me with it. I got signed out without ever getting signed out. Mama took me to the car and fussed all the way home on how I was going to hell for singing the devil's music, how God wasn't pleased with what I did, and if I didn't use the talent He gave me for himself, I would lose the gift altogether.

I was so sad that my mama did that to me for the whole school to see. I was also very shocked. She never lies. If she says she's gonna do something, you'd better believe she's gonna do just what she says. And if she says she's NOT going to do something, you can take it to the bank. But this time, I gave the performance of my life, pulled on her heartstrings, and I got just what I deserved.

I was terrified to get on the bus the next morning. I didn't feel like the ridicule from what was done. I was silent when I boarded. Everyone on the bus clapped for me and told me how great I sounded. They still laughed at what they called the best comedy show with Mama snatching me from a seated position for the grand finale. Some even thought it was staged.

Later in the day, the winners were to be announced over the intercom. I knew I was disqualified for leaving campus without permission and for not finishing because Mama snatched me off the piano in the climax of my performance.

They started with third place, then second, then the best overall. Whose name did they call for best overall? My name. I was in utter shock.

I went to the office to collect my prize. It was a check for 100 smackers! Wow, I had actually won. Unbelievable.

I went home. My mama was there. I rushed to my bookbag to show her the envelope. I said, "Mama, look. See? I won the talent show. They gave me a check for winning too."

"Lemme see dat." Looking at the envelope, she agreed with me by reading my name on the package. Then she opened it up, investigating it further to discover the check was legitimate from my school. She read my name again on the pay to the order of... "Yep, dat's your name on the check, and yep that's one hundid dollars." Then the most outrageous thing happened. She tore up the check

42

into pieces. *WHAT? I need that hundred dollars right now.* Mama said, "You'll never spend dat dey money. That's de devil money! In this house, we don't serve the devil; we serve GOD! Don't you ever forget dat!"

Money did not mean a thing to my mama for the lesson. I didn't get it (the money), but I got it (the lesson and the sacrifice).

THE MOTHER'S DAY GIFT I WASN'T
PREPARED FOR

I was 16 years old when I started receiving company from a boy. He worked as an orderly for the hospital. He was friends with my brother's wife. He had seen me a few times at the hospital as a patient and as a visitor. He started calling and from there, he started coming over at two-hour intervals. Mama allowed him to visit every other Tuesday night and every other Saturday afternoon. It was nice. I would sing and play the piano for him, and we would laugh and talk about nothing.

It was approaching Mother's Day. I was getting a weekly allowance from my parents. I had planned to go shopping with Daddy to get my mama a present. Willie, my beau, came to see me that Saturday. We had a very good visit. He asked me had I gone shopping for Mother's Day and I replied, "Not yet, but my daddy will be taking me."

The next thing he said was so kind, I just couldn't believe it. As he leaned to the left to retrieve his wallet from his back pocket, he opened the wallet and pulled out a five-dollar bill and said, "Put this with what you have to give her a really special gift."

"Aw, that's so sweet." I went back in my fencing rules book because I was never to take money from a man. But this time, it wasn't for me, it was for my mama. I looked at him (in case motive was plastered on his face) and the only thing I could see was pride of a working man being generous to his little girlfriend for her mother. No other motive.

I put the money in my purse and hid the information from Mama. About 2:00 a.m., Mama came and woke me up singing, "Get up. Get up, child. The Holy Ghost woke me up and told me that something in your wallet I need to see."

I'm thinking with great alarm, "MONEY, MONEY!" I got very suspicious, thinking, "Ain' no Holy Ghost tell you 'bout my wallet. You were eavesdropping through a drinking glass on the other side of the wall, listening to our conversation." I'm also thinking that Mama is old and fat with little legs. I am a track runner and youth is definitely on my side. I could outrun her, snatch the money out before she catches up with me, but the quicker I moved, she was right on my heel. I lied and said, "I think I lost my wallet or left it at school." She came back with, "Dah wallet is here. The Lord woke me up for you to show me what's in it. Get it and get it right now!"

In the parlor was a desk. The right side of the desk had three drawers, which was my side. I got there before Mama and pulled out so many things before I got to the green plastic money purse. I was trying to get the money out before she saw it. But when she saw a glimpse of it, she moved in on me and snatched it out of my hand, looked in it, and said, "AH-HA! What is dis? Way you get dis money from? Me and ya daddy ain' give you no money yet. So way you git it from?"

I stuttered because I was so nervous, but I swallowed deep, took in a deep breath, and said, "This is for your Mother's Day present. Willie asked me if I had gone shopping for your gift and I told him, 'Not yet,' so he gave me $5 to put with what I would buy for you, Mama. It was never for me. It was for you. Isn't that nice? He's very thoughtful, right, Mama?"

"You lying heifer. You knew what he was up to. If he wanted to give me a present, he sho' didn't give it to me. I told you never to take money from a man. When he come yere Tuesday, I got something for him. Donchu answer no more of his calls, ya hear me?"

Crying and heartbroken, I said, "Yes, ma'am." I couldn't understand why it was wrong to be thoughtful and kind to someone's mama. Maybe he only had a grandmama.

I couldn't talk to him Sunday or Monday. He was scheduled to come on Tuesday at 7:00 and stay until 9:00.

When the doorbell rang, Mama told me not to answer the door that she'd get it. It was indeed Willie coming to take company with me. Mama answered the door, telling him, "Nena mind your hat."

Willie was somewhat of a stutterer, especially when he was nervous. Mama asked him for his intent for her child. He was trying to answer, but she latched in on another question before he could answer the former question.

"When boys give girls money, dey be looking for something in return. Did you give my child some money?"

Nervously stammering, "Y-y-yes, ma'am."

"And you was looking for something in return, whatn' you?"

"Y-y-yes, ma'am."

"I knew it. You can't fool me. Well, here is your $5. You take it and don't you dart my door no mo!"

Dating life was over. My mama canned that and that was that! He never called anymore and would not receive any calls from me.

I was in college when I saw him again. He was heartbroken over what Mama did. He told me he was so nervous, he was answering, "Yes, ma'am," even when he really didn't understand the line of questioning. It was like being on the *Perry Mason* TV Show. He told me he meant no harm and I should have told him that wasn't a good idea. He also told me he eventually moved on, he had a new girlfriend, and was planning to be married in another year.

NO FREE MOVIE

Mama was Grandma to her son's first two children. I was Auntie. I loved the prestige of being an aunt. I loved them and I loved playing with them. Their imagination and sense of seeing things were so entertaining. Mama thought it was a good idea for me to keep my nephew and niece. They were small, in their single digits, and I was a teen. I was not being paid like those who babysit, but I was getting training and I liked being useful and needed.

One day, when asked to keep up with my tribe, I said, "Gladly." I told my little tribe that we would all take a nap and when we wake, we would have a show in the living room or do something very fun. I was known for having fun. They were no more than five and I was no more than 14 or 15.

I had a conflict in my head while playing with the kids before our nap. I had this great idea to go to the movies. By this time, we'd gotten rid of the color film that white folks sold door-to-door to black folks to go over their TVs so they can say they have a colored screen. It was presented so well to the homemakers or domestic workers who saw colored TVs in their buckers' houses that they made a killing. Those little ridiculously despicable screens had three colors: blue for the sky, reddish-yellow for the people's faces, and green for the ground. The neighborhood gladly purchased one or two. Each screen costed $20. When my parents got tired of the fake look, they upgraded to a real color floor model console TV. This made me happy. It also made me want to go see one of Disney's films at the movies I'd seen on the TV commercial.

When I thought the kids were fast asleep, I took off by myself to go downtown. I was so nervous...not about the children, but about me. I had never really gone anywhere by myself, except to catch the bus for school and that was just around the corner, or the time I took flight on foot as fast as I could to the downtown infirmary because my daddy was at the brink of death and fear was nowhere to be found.

I was going to walk by myself. Me, the girl, who in years past got hit by a car coming home from school. I was nervous. *What if I have an aura or a trigger and a seizure comes on me? Would anybody know what to do to help me?* But my ambition overrode my fear and I started out on my adventure. I didn't consider the kids would wake. Well, I did think they could, so I locked them in the den and took the key so they couldn't get out and hurt themselves before I returned. Since I'd never gone to a movie, I was thinking it was like our color TV (the show is free, it's over in an hour, and all will be well). I already knew I couldn't talk to strangers and not to get in the car with anyone, even if I knew them. I was quick on my feet because I ran track and I loved running.

When I got to the downtown theater, I felt so accomplished. This could go on my résumé for when I needed to go somewhere for Mama, go visit my aunts, or even do the movie trip again. I didn't take any money because ain' nobody told me the movies weren't free. At home on the color set, the shows and movies were free, drinks and snacks were free, so it was not even a consideration.

I got to the window and announced the movie I wanted to see, expecting her to let me in. The first thing she asked me was, "Where's your parent?"

"At work," I said.

"$1," she told me.

"Oh, I can't get in? I wanted to see the movie. I don't have any money."

Asking for money from anyone, especially a man, was an absolute no-no.

"Well, you can't get in without a ticket. So go on back home. Go straight back home."

I was so disappointed. As I got closer to home on Rush Street, I saw a commotion near my house. Then I saw the ambulance, my mama and daddy's car, my nephew, niece, and our next-door neighbor, Mrs. Sawyer. Oh, boy! Here we go!

The children were crying profusely because they were locked in the room and they could not find me. The neighbor heard the children and knocked on the door. She imagined me having a seizure and was out cold or dead, so she called the police, the ambulance…and you guessed it, my parents.

My little tribe was so glad to see me that they ran to greet me and then they beat me with their little fists while crying because I scared them deeply. They were glad to see that I was alright. Mrs. Sawyer scolded me as if I was her child. My daddy gave me the tongue lashing of my life. I had everybody so worried. I never considered that. I didn't think it through. What am I saying? I didn't think. I just wanted to go to the movies to see the show.

The first responders saw that I was alright, in big trouble, but alright. Well, Mama waited until everyone had gone back to their respective places. Mama and I went back and forth. Yes, we all had a conversation that day.

"I'm sorry, Mama. I ain' gon do it no mo."

"I know you ain' gon do it no mo cause you shud'nah done it to start wid."

The children watched as Mama wore me out with the belt on the refrigerator. The strap was named Uncle Sankim. The children laughed at me and they too were sad for me.

From that day to a long time after, I never wanted to go to the

49

movies again, especially knowing the show, popcorn, and candy weren't free.

WORDS DO MATTER

As a young tike,[7] I always took people at face value. I was influenced by their words and language of their bodies. Commercials I heard on the radio and television had a great impression on me.

In the 60s, there were two schools of commercials on smoking. One commercial, the slogan was, "I'd rather fight than switch." For the woman, it was very cool to have a cigarette between your fingers, puffing, and blowing. For the man, it showed him in control, powerful, and desirable if he was smoking a cigarette or just holding it between his fingers. Smoking commercials showed people at parties, restaurants, the pool, driving, riding, and so on and so forth.

I don't think Daddy ever smoked in the house, but on occasion, I would see him camping out in the yard, in the toolshed, or standing over his really old 1944 green Chevrolet with a cigar in his mouth trying to figure out the answer to his vehicular problem.

The other commercial was about the nicotine found in cigarettes and smoking cigarettes could cause cancer. They were at some point called cancer sticks. Daddy was my everything. Thinking about him dying from something that he could control and avoid gave me the heebie-jeebies. I wanted to tell him, but thinking about it gave me great fear. I thought and thought about him and smoking and said to myself, "I'm just a child. My words won't have any power."

One Saturday mid-afternoon, Mama was still at work and Daddy was outside mowing the grass. When I heard the mower sounds, I came out to watch him and to be near him. He had the cigar in his mouth, with smoke coming off the lit end. I took courage and boldness, almost like an adult. Love took me over and I said, "Daddy, please don't smoke that cigar. They are bad for you. They will kill you. I

---

[7] A small child

51

love you, Daddy. I don't want you to die. I don't want you to smoke." Then I sealed the deal with a big hug and squeeze. My height didn't matter. My scrawny little self squeezed him with all my might as my head landed somewhere between his stomach and chest. In that powerful moment, he took the cigar, threw it down to the ground, and crushed it with his foot.

My daddy died at 83, but from that day in the yard when I spoke to him about smoking, to the very day he died, he never smoked again, not even in secret. So, it does matter what you say to another human being. Ain' nobody told me my words had power.

THE DAY MY MAMA STOOD UP FOR ME

Some of the greatest events of Mama's and my relationship were far and few between, but there were some treasured moments that were my all-time favorites. She and I would frequent Woolworth/Kress (a five and dime store uptown) on Saturdays just to stimulate the economy and to change the scenery of our mundane lives. She as a domestic worker, and me as a student. On this particular morning, Mama did her shopping as I watched her pick up brands that were either important to her or brands she could afford. When done, she and I got in the checkout line. This would be my very first time experiencing racism. I've noticed the separate everything, but my parents had the higher power of dealing with it. They knew what to do to shield me from the repercussions that came along with being subhuman.

While we were waiting for our turn, Mama thought about the White Rose hair grease. I was old enough to remember where it was located and was sent to get a jar while she held the line. As I was returning to Mama, I politely walked through other customers in line, saying, "Excuse me," nodding, and smiling to get to her, when abruptly an old man, who was about the third or fourth customer behind Mama thought I was trying to jump the line and jump in front of him.

He was dressed in cowboy gear. He had the hat, the bolo necktie, and the pointed toe cowboy boots. You could tell he was from another place. He looked like a mock Colonel Sanders or a big Texan cowboy president. He snatched me by my right arm with venom and said, "Where you think you going, Nigga?" This was something I NEVER saw my mama do. She put both hands forward toward the man, shaking them, and somewhat stuttering, saying, "It's okay, Mista. She wid me." She started to lower her body and to shrink or cow down. She beckoned for me and he let me go. Mama snatched me near her side. I was safe. Mama was safe. That was really scary, but Mama was amazing. We never spoke of that incident that day or any day after.

FINE CHINA

Mama had a fetish for pretty things, such as pitchers and goblet sets. She had many tea sets, pitcher sets, and glasses in abundance. She took me to an antique store one day. Her eyes fell on a blue antique five-piece goblet and pitcher set. She asked my opinion and I responded according to its beauty. Mama made the purchase. The clerk took her time and wrapped each goblet and placed it in a brown paper bag with a strong paper rope handle. Mama was careful carrying it to the car.

When we got home, she filled up the sink with hot water, got a little bleach and dish detergent to carefully wash the set, in preparation for its new home. She then displayed her new *trophies* in the china cabinet.

The pastor of my mama's church came for an occasional dinner with a few other guests. Not to my surprise, one of the centerpieces on the table was the blue pitcher. Later that year, I was going to be turning 13. I slipped into my courage enough to ask if we could have a party using the heavy antique blue five-piece pitcher and goblet set. I wanted that feeling of specialness as I poured out my favorite grape flavored Kool-Aid beverage. I was shocked when Mama said, "Yes," and I'm sure she was equally as shocked when I asked.

Six years later, when I was 19, I did the DUM DUM DEE DUMB thing. Yes, I went on the word of my mama and married the man she coerced me or strongly suggested that I marry since he looked like he liked me. (Mama was afraid I'd be an old maid.) I didn't know him longer than a New York minute. We met at college and he chased and pursued me. Although we courted two days a week at Mama's house and every day that we saw each other on campus for six months, I had no inkling of what life would be like married. We spent time together. I met his family, he went with me to church a few times, and we talked over the phone a lot, but in my opinion, it wasn't enough to say, "I do." We knew nothing about each other. If you don't know what a thing is or who someone is, you are most likely or liable to get entangled with it repeatedly. We had simple blowups and we kissed a lot. When he asked me for my most sacred gift, I told him, "Until you say I do, I don't!" My mama and the church taught us not to commit adultery or fornication. In essence, "Keep your drawers up and your dress down, and you won't have a baby."

When we got married, Mama upgraded and purchased new furniture and gave me the pieces I was familiar with. She told me to choose what I wanted in the house. She made sure I obliged. That was special. I chose the heavy oak rocking chair I grew up rocking in. It was my comforter many days and nights.

In the first grade, I couldn't get the alphabets right, so my teacher arranged for a student teacher (Miss Hennigan) to help me with my numbers and ABCs. She taught me quite a few ways, but one day one of her techniques clicked. I got it! I had it down pat. I was so happy and I wanted to savor the moment. So to celebrate the feat, I got a safety pin and carved my ABCs into Mama's bedroom furniture so she could see firsthand my accomplishment. I had no clue of its value, so I went for the dresser. The expensive dresser to be exact. It was mahogany wood and had clawed dresser drawers. It was the real McCoy. I was extremely ecstatic about my accomplishments and got my mama to help me celebrate. When she saw what I did, she beat my bottom, saying, I ruined her furniture. I thought she would be happy I knew how to write my alphabets.

She then gladly gave me the trophy bedroom suit, along with many other cosmetic things like curtains, tablecloths, sheets, pots, dishes, glasses, etc. I felt so loved and special 'til I went a little further. I was feeling froggy on that instance by asking for her silver tea server. Obviously, I had crossed the line. "You can forget that. You ain' gon have my tea server," she said matter-of-factly. That being said, I figured it would be of no use to ask about the blue antique pitcher and goblet set from my 13th birthday celebration. I was very happy about my new pieces for our new home with my new husband, Burk Jaimas.

On Christmas that year, my mama gave me a gift-wrapped present. It was a big package…heavy too. I tore into it with anticipation and excitement, only to discover the five-piece blue antique pitcher and goblet set. I felt ultimate joy. I sensed my mama knew how much that meant to me. Maybe that was her plan all the time, but what was certain was that the set was passed down to me! I was joyous about this gift from her at such a pivotal time in my life.

The institution of marriage and the institution of parenthood are supposed to be the ultimate joy. I was in love with the idea of being in love and being a mother. One of my good friends told me after eight years of marriage, "Girl, you know you're not happy." I was appalled with her observance, but what was true was I had tricked myself into thinking I was happy as a coping mechanism. I think I hid from my own self. I was in denial…the cuss-outs, the lack of money, the beatings, the threats with guns, and the many nights alone as he made drug runs.

He didn't have a cake walk with me either as his wife. He had to contend with the little girl camouflaged as a woman, the many illnesses (mental and physical), seizures, depression, headaches, the lack of not knowing my birth mother, the loneliness, and three children…on top of all the other issues.

At first, I ran to music for help and he ran to drugs and alcohol for help. As life became more problematic, I started having extramarital affairs and he turned to more drugs, violence, and alcohol just to cope. I had absolutely no self-worth, so I went deeper into loathing by masturbation, mutilation, and kleptomania. The more oppressed and mentally sick I felt, the more the symptoms reacted with ailments that kept me at the lowest state. I was usually perplexed. What a vicious cycle to be plagued with.

The day I thought I would die was the Sunday I fell on the porch of my home with a grand malfunction in my brain. The hospital report said I had more than 20 seizures. I was unconscious for many days. I was also pregnant with our youngest son, K. I wasn't doing well, and I wanted to go where Jesus was, since I could get no real healing for my body and mind.

God spoke to my little frail spirit and said He would not take me because I must finish my assignments. My first assignments were self-perseverance and the ministry of motherhood. I needed to be intact and I needed to mother my children. I needed them and they needed me. I cried, begged, and pleaded just to see His face. He was adamant. In fact, He spoke no more about it.

Prior to K being born, the doctors had given us a grim outlook. They said because I lost a lot of oxygen during the seizure episodes, they believed he could even be stillborn or severely retarded. But that wasn't what happened. When he came out of me, he was another perfect being from the imagination of God. He weighed 6 lbs., 2 oz., and was 18 inches long, with slanted eyes. He was diagnosed with two separate syndromes: Trisomy 21 (an extra chromosome, the 'Down's Syndrome') and Cyanosis (the 'blue lips syndrome'). They could not explain if that was a result of the many seizures I had or another reason. Poor oxygen circulation in the blood caused the bluish discoloration of the skin because of the lower levels of oxygen in the red blood cells. Central cyanosis affected K's tongue and lips.

The doctors warned me to keep him wrapped in two blankets at all times or he could die. They told me to put my child in a home because he was a Mongoloid child. "He has the Down's Syndrome and he will be mentally retarded. It will be difficult raising him with your other children." I was very firm, saying, "I AM gonna put him in a home…MY HOME! That's my child!"

Having my children were the best events that EVER happened to me. We loved each other as if each one of us were GOD. Our relationship as a young mother to my children and vice versa was perfect. There was NO condition to our love. It was AGAPE! Although there were health challenges, a lack of money, food, essential things, and a dad/husband (at times), we made it quite successfully, even through the intellectual challenges. K was not the only one riding that train. We all had challenges in that arena. The challenge started with me as a dyslexic. My sons had challenges with numbers, reading, and writing. Amazingly, I had the gift of words and sound. I sounded very educated because I am an audible learner. I love music. I love sound. I love words. I gave this gift to all of my children. My sons' first teacher was me. I might have taught my left handed, upside-down vision of 'Nita Learning.' I learned differently and I taught differently.

The acceptance of a slightly less than perfect child with special needs sent their dad into a head spin of events that looked like rage, denial, and depression. He was not just dealing with the imperfect child, but the loss of his mother the day after Easter in the early 80s really took its toll on him.

Mama said if you make your bed hard, you gotta live in it. That was a hard pill to swallow because I didn't get a proper education in marital life as a young person. I didn't know about having babies or any grown-up things. I was totally naïve. Since I got whippings from Mama just about every week about something, when this charged up man started his threats with guns and hurting our sons physically and emotionally, I thought this was what it was supposed to be like. I never saw that in my upbringing, but my parents were old and they might have done all the sinner things already. Their initial job was to train the child, break the child, beat the child, and all of these fit under the umbrella called love. Assuredly, church didn't teach me any better about friends, life, love, parenthood, money, bills, etc. Nope! Just bring your burdens and your money to the LORD and leave them there!

One October night, in the early 80s, the man I married said to me while cleaning his Smith & Wesson nickel Magnum 357 gun, "I could kill you right now. No one would know, and no one would care. Nobody wants you with all these children, with your seizure sickness. Shoot, I barely want you myself!"

I made up in my mind that Halloween night that if I woke up the next morning and I wasn't dead, I was going to take my children and I was leaving this man! When he went to work, I woke the children, got some clothes together, and left. I was never going to return. Unfortunately, I didn't use the best smarts that day when I went back to grab some more stuff and he caught me there. I had to think fast and use the smarts to get out without getting seriously or fatally injured.

He asked me, "Where do you think you're going?"

I said, "There is a lady in my church who is really going through and I want to be a blessing to her."

He didn't know that I was really talking about myself. I had some blankets, lamps, and food in my hand.

"I know GOD would be pleased with me to help out a sister in a time of need," I told him.

Not sure of what he was going to say, but he went for it, and I got in Old Beulah, my daddy's 1972 Blue Park Avenue, and drove off. My children were with a close friend from the country.

THE ART OF INNOCENCE

I have always loved the beauty of colors (bold or pastels). Once, when my mama and I went to Woolworth/Kress, coloreds were watched like hawks for trying on clothing or assuming we were stealing. We were treated inhumane at their small lunch counter. Such non-privileged actions, while they still screamed for us to giv'um our money.

Well, one Friday, I wanted to look in the paper section of the store while my mother was getting her shopping done. I wanted a little independence to look around. I was drawn to the paper aisle. It was filled with colored construction paper, colored notebooks, pastel notepads, sticky notes, and all that a tween who loved pretty papers could envision. I was in colored paper heaven. I wanted a plastic box of small note pastel papers. I picked it up and ran to my mama so she could buy it for me. I needed it. I could feel smart and useful with this tightly-wrapped paper. I was abruptly awakened by Mama's reality.

"Gal, if you don't go and put that mess back. You don't need that! Didn't I jess buy you some paper lass week?"

"No, Mama. That was notebook paper. This is better and it has lots of color. Please, Mama, may I have it?"

"Didchu hear what I say? I said go and put dem people stuff back."

Heartbroken, I resigned and went very slowly back to the paper aisle to return it back on the shelf, when suddenly I had a brilliant idea! I was wearing my little green shoulder pocketbook and nothing was in it but a pencil from school and some chewing gum. It had the right amount of space for the colored notepads. I looked to my left, then to my right, and I saw NO ONE. I inconspicuously unzipped the top of my shoulder bag and took a deep breath to be fast and quick.

I slipped the pads in my bag, squinted my shoulders and eyes, and waited for something bad to happen. No one said anything because no one saw me. I was scot free. After a few long moments, I hightailed it back to Mama. It felt like eternity from the time I put them in my pocketbook until I was home in my room. All while in the vehicle, I was waiting for my mama to beat me for taking the pads. She always said, "I got eyes in the back of my head. If you took it, I'll know it."

"Hmm, she didn't see me," I thought to myself.

But ain' nobody told me NOT to be stupid. Ain' nobody told me NOT to put the used paper in the trash can.

Monday morning rolled around and I had to be at school. I was feeling pretty good about myself because I outsmarted my mama, who was heaven's candidate for sniffing out wrong. I took my precious notepads to school to continue feeling smart and important. No one knew and I didn't tell. Oh, but when I got home from school, my mama met me at the front door with my wastepaper basket. And what was in the basket? You already know.

"Needah."

"Yes, ma'am."

"Way you got dis paper from? Ain' dat the paper I told you whatn' gon get? I know I didn't give you no money to get it, so how you got it?"

Those questions didn't require an answer; they were strictly rhetorical. She answered herself for me. "You stole it, you old heifer. You going to hell. You know dah Bible say, 'Thou shall not steal.' 'Cuz if you steal, you'll lie; and if you lie, you'll cheat; and if you cheat, you'll kill; and if you kill, den you done broke all the commandments."

Before she went at me for the whipping, I started in on the crying for sympathy. Of course, it did NO GOOD. She committed to teaching me a lesson with the rod of correction, Uncle Sankim. That's right! She wore me out good. Then on that same Monday, she took me back to the store. I had to tell the management I took their product, ask him for forgiveness, pay the store because I used it, and in humiliation, pray in front of my mama and the manager. All who were looking were snickering at me. Wow! What a way to learn a lesson.

THE ART OF STEALING

The next event was a little more intense. It was in my daddy's toolshed. I would be in there with him on many occasions and one day I noticed a large wooden chest with a lock on it. Immediately, I pictured him as a rich pirate. I knew where he kept the key to the toolshed. One day after school, I got the key, went to the shed as if it were my own, opened it, and went straight for the treasure chest. I could not get it open. I was so excited to know he was a real live rich pirate. I expected to see gold, jewelry for Christmas, and money, money, money! My daddy was ALWAYS my hero, so it's no wonder he was rich with lots of treasure like the KING, Jesus.

I used every key on the chain to unlock the chest. None of them worked. I had to find a way to get in. There were so many people I wanted to help too.

I was in the second grade. I had the brilliant idea to use a protractor to open the lock of the chest. And what do you know, I fumbled and tackled; I aimed and pushed and shoved until at last it was open.

My eyes could barely take it in. There were coins upon coins upon coins. I yelled in excitement, "My daddy's rich!"

I began to make my list of the friends I would help. Maybe I had a sense of entitlement or a bit of braggadociousness. Whatever the emotion, it was pure.

I ran to the house, pulled some Dixie paper cups down from the dispenser, and ran back to the shed with the opened chest. I filled up about three little cups of coins, concealed them in my bookbag for school the next day, and closed the chest up after smoothing it over with my hand so it wouldn't look interrupted. I locked the toolshed back as if I had never been in there before, ever.

I don't even remember who I gave the cups to. I only remember who approached me to bring her a cup. I said to Marcha, "You don't even like me. Why would I bring you something nice if you're always mean to me?"

"I won't be mean to you anymore if you bring me some money tomorrow."

I was so happy to have her as my new friend that I hugged her and told her I would bring her a cup of money. We escaped the eyes of the teacher that day. I was sound and clear of trouble. I was doing the work of a little missionary like in our church. I felt good about it.

THE BUBBLE-BURSTER

Marcha bursted my bubble and messed it up for everyone, but literally saved my life. She lived right around the corner from us and was usually a little mean spirited. She called my mama's house almost bedtime that fateful Monday night.

"Hello, may I speak to Nita?"

My mama answered the phone with, "Who is dis?"

"This Marcha."

"Nita don't answer no phone dis time a night. What you want with her anyhow?"

"Tell her don't forget to bring my money tomorrow."

"Bring your money? Nita ain' got no job to bring you no money. Hang up dis phone!"

I remember it as if it were this morning. Mama came at me with, "Whah some gal got business calling here saying you 'pose to give her some money? Way you get money from to give to other people?"

I was so excited to tell Mama that Daddy wasn't just a deacon or a railroad man, he's a real live rich pirate.

"I found his treasure chest in the toolshed. It's filled with money to help the poor. I gave some friends some money yesterday."

"You telling me you got money from the trunk in the shed?"

"No, ma'am. It's not a trunk; it's a treasure chest. It's filled with money."

66

"That trunk was locked and you broke in it and took the church money. Ah, you going to hell for stealing the CHURCH MONEY! I betcha your daddy gon cut that tail when he gets off work!"

Mama could barely wait to tell him about my situation. He was in shock and in disbelief when he found out. He asked me how much did I give out. I said three paper cups full. He said I would have to pay that back. His lesson to me was, "Anything you want, you can have, but you gotta ask for anything you want. We take care of you 'round here. If it ain' worth asking for, den it ain' worth having. Money in dah bank and it's yours, but you can't just go get it. You gotta ask somebody for it. You understand?"

His tongue lashing was tempered with lovingkindness, and no, I didn't get a beating for that incident.

THE INNOCENCE OF STEALING

Even though my parents would never agree with the ideology that I was an abused person, many of my peers and others did. Not only was I, but I became the abuser to my precious children. I remember for one of my children (and he let me know his painful account), I pulled the fish tank line out of the water and whipped his bottom for something that really didn't fit the crime. I used various objects to make my point valid. I demanded respect. Then I would try to turn those events into something loving (in my eyes) by baking cookies and buttering up to my children so they could know I completely loved them, didn't want to hurt them, and was just training them against doing wrong.

I vividly remember calling the police on my five-year-old because he took a toy car from the shelf of the Kroger-Savon, then lied about it when asked. When he took the toy, I was nervous he was going to turn out like his klepto-mama, so I called the police on him, and NO, I didn't think it was an overreaction. I had ALL boys, and life was never kind to the black boy or the black man. I had to use drastic measures.

Here was this cute, but terrified little boy, who knew to protect himself with the best lie he could come up with. "My daddy bought it for me." "My teacher gave it to me." "I always had it." I had to give him the lesson on stealing and how wrong that was, so I called the police to have him picked up (not arrested) and driven around the neighborhood to give him some true facts about jail and how he could wind up dead from poor choices.

I was the hypocrite with great intentions for my sons. I did the very same thing at the same store. I took a very pretty compact from the shelf of the cosmetic aisle, and no, I was not five. I was 25 or so.

The worst part of the whole thing was I left my children in our black Monte Carlo car to wait until I returned. The truth of the matter was, I didn't get out without being caught. I didn't know I was being watched. I did buy some items, but the pretty thing gave me a thrill and a pleasure to take it. I sure didn't need it. I was just getting high on the thrill. I was sent upstairs to see the management team. I talked and cried my way out of that scary situation. Only GOD kept me from getting arrested, having me openly exposed with my name and face in the daily newspaper, and my kids from going to DSS for placement. I knew better because my mama was adamant about rogues.

When I finally got to the car (without the compact), I hugged and kissed all three of them as if I was seeing them for the first time. I took us home, which was moments away, and cooked us a Sunday meal to celebrate my private victory. Did that stop me from stealing again? It did not! I continued taking cute little inconspicuous things until I finally got it all out of my system.

THE CHUCKTOWN HOTTIE

I did dumb stuff like tell the older boys I would pick them up from school, knowing full well, I was not going to be in town. I was flirting with a man slightly older than my boys. I was all in with this young whippersnapper.

The strange thing was, when my boy went on his booty call at 15, I called the preacher and the policeman for intervention for him; but it was the same crime I had done with that whippersnapper. I was a young, untrained child trying to play out life the best I could, while trying to be a Christian woman.

I did many things in the name of love to, for, with, and against my children that I am not proud of.

What if my mom was the exact same way, hoping to be this picture-perfect person, but the reality was, she was a despicable human being who could cook her way into your heart, and life was good?

THE WORD "MOTHER"

This was another day when I discovered the tender mercies of my daddy. It certainly could have gone a different way. I was in the fourth grade. While in class, these dark-skinned paternal twins came into our class in the middle of the school term. They seemed nice, but they talked a lot. One day at recess, they were fussing and just being mean. They spoke about their mother so often, until it just laid on your brain, and you would be compelled to repeat it.

After school that same day, I came home and got on my bike. Gloria, my neighbor and classmate, came over to play. She wanted to take a turn riding my bike. I didn't really want to share my bike that day, at that particular time, so I said, "No" and called her a mother@#$^*! She knew! However, I didn't know. She responded with, "Ooh, I'mma tell your mama and your daddy you said a bad word. You gonna get a beating." Everyone in the neighborhood knew I had a strict upbringing because my parents were extreme disciplinarians. My mama's nickname was Adolf Hitler.

I comforted Gloria and assured her that was NOT a cuss word. *Children do not cuss. Donnie says it all the time. No one ever said he was bad, or he was using cuss words.* So I used the word again to show it wasn't a bad word. Gloria repeated, "You said it again? Ooh, you know you gonna get a beating this time with the quickness."

I obstinately refused to believe what she was saying. To prove to her once and for all it was a great word, I took her by the hand and led her to my daddy's man cave (the toolshed). I opened my mouth and said, "Daddy, ain' mother@#$^*! a good word?" The gentle and kind man, who was the deacon of his church, a railroad mechanic, and nobody's pushover, gave me a look of disbelief and horror. He had a cigar between his lips and a hammer and some nails in his hand fixing something of value to him. When he heard the question, he snatched the cigar from his mouth and said, "Hot toe Motor

Desoto."[8] I was not alarmed because I was so confident of the nature of the word. However, he had a slightly different view. He had a change to his voice as he asked me, "Where did you get such a word? Dat dey is some of the most nastiest cussing you could ever hear!" I explained about the new twins who came to our class always used the term on the playground and even under their breath.

While in the company of my friend, Daddy took me to his knee for me to sit. He told me that was not a good word and asked if I ever heard him or my mama use that word. I replied, "No" to both questions. He said if I'd never heard anyone from church or our house use certain words, then I should never use the word either. I was so shocked. I could not believe mother@#$^*! was a profane word. How could it be? It had the word "mother" in it. Mothers are nice, kind, smart, pretty, godly, and caring.

He looked me straight in the eye, shook his head, and spoke that the Lord should help me and have mercy on me. I was that literal speaker and thinker. That day, he gave me a pass because I obviously never heard the word before the twins had come along, but I had been duly warned never to think on the word or speak the word ever again, even as an adult, or else!

Well, Gloria's plan to see me in a bad situation did not play out in her favor. That was a great moment for me. When out of my daddy's view, I curved my body and licked my tongue at her to celebrate me and mock her for such a vicious idea to start with. I never spoke of the word again until my first Richard Pryor movie.

---

[8] Daddy's way of cussing

BURK, CARRIE, AND I

In the mid-80s, I didn't really have a handle on life outside high school, church, the grocery store, and my music. My parents prepared me for church, but I wasn't prepared for life outside of their home or the bubble called church. Burk chose me in college and six months later, we were wed. Although I had some college, a marriage, three children, and a few friends, I was the naïvest child trying to learn adulthood. There is much I could say about my messed-up situation, but that's another chapter in another book.

I was feeling pretty alone by the time all our children were born because he didn't rush right home most days. He worked for a chair factory and he was into his friends still. So, I would pass the time by bonding and playing with our children. They were human dolls to me. I loved the sound of their giggles. Being with them and watching them play, sleep, and eat was better than watching television. None of these notions weren't far-fetched, being I was childlike too.

It was the first week of my birthday month. I wanted to do something new, different, and adventurous. I wanted to be noticed, feel appreciated, and loved. It was about time for Burk to get home from work. I heard wood chopping in the back, so I peeked out the window and there was Carrie, Burk's friend, who would occasionally come over when he was in town. He knocked on the back door to take some of the wood inside. It's like he saw there was no chopped wood for the greyish-black potbelly stove in the living room. In about 40 minutes, Burk came in from the factory. They greeted each other, and Burk greeted me with a kiss. Carrie gently started the 'Bruh, you slipping around the house' conversation to his friend, saying things like, "You shouldn't leave the house without preparing proper heating for your family, and I just happened to look in the fridge and there wasn't enough food for the family. Dude, c'mon!"

Wow, I knew they were army comrades, but I didn't know he could say those things. Burk felt bad. I could tell, but I secretly felt amazing that someone other than my daddy was sticking up for the children and me, and that was without me ever opening my mouth! He said to Burk, "Nita's birthday is coming up soon. I know you gonna do something wonderful for her, but I want to take her to the movies. You stay home with the kids. She's always with these kids."

The most incredible thing happened. Who do you know would accept this as good? Burk and I were really stupid that day. He agreed with his friend and said I deserved a good movie. I felt so special that day.

In a couple of weeks, Carrie came to the house after Burk was home from work. I had seen the movie trailer for Richard Pryor now showing. I was ecstatic because he was the funniest guy on television. I needed some comic relief. I was sooooooo excited because I had never been to the movies in my whole life. Well, except the time I tried to get in the movies without a parent or money.

Well, ain' nobody told me that outside of TV, he was the most vulgar comedian ever. I heard words, conversations, and vividly described scenes I could never imagine. I laughed some. I was embarrassed a lot more. There were so many visuals and so much profanity.

After the movie was over, Carrie asked if I wanted to go to dinner. I said, "No, I cooked already." On the way home, we talked about the movie and he brought up more points that he'd seen in his friend not being a good provider, and the continuous drinking and pot smoking. I felt somewhat validated. So when I got home, I repeated some of the things Carrie said. Along with that, I thought I would bring up, with the passion of Richard Pryor, a few choice cuss words. Burk took a look at me, tilted his head like a canine, and asked me, "Whachu trying to say, woman? You cussing now? (blurting out in

74

laughter) You don't know how to cuss, girl. Those cuss words don't even go together! You sound so funny right now."

That sort of ended my cussing career. But the damage was done as Carrie enticed me to go with him. He threatened Burk. He told him he would take me away from him if he didn't straighten up and take care of his family, and that he would buy me a house and give me the finer things I deserved. This was all so flattering for a low self-esteemed, young married woman with toddlers and a bunch of health issues. This was all so dangerous for the three of us. We all could have died that day. Burk had a gun named Josephine. However, his guilt made him cry because he wasn't giving me the best of himself.

THE DINNER THEATER

Since nothing happened that day, I sighed with relief. Still, I took a chance further. In less than a week, I was asked to come to Virginia and meet Carrie for a Live Dinner Theater. Wow, with the exception of a few high school dramas, I had never, ever seen a live dinner theater before. I was thrilled to be going back home where I lived for a season as a child.

I called my cousin ahead to ask if I could hang out a few days with my son at her place. She agreed we needed to catch up. I told Burk I was going to my cousin's house in Virginia to show off our baby, to catch up, and to get some serious rest. He was okay with what I said. I felt something was quite challenging with that. *Why wasn't he questioning me about being away from the house for any period of time?* I never revealed my intent to go with Carrie, nor did he question me any further. I thought he'd be inquisitive at least. Perhaps he didn't want to stir up the nest because, just maybe, he could have his own freedoms without conflict or false guilt.

Carrie bought tickets to the show, the train fare, and booked me a hotel room in the city of Hampton. 'Hello, Dolly!' was the feature. What I didn't know was he booked only one room. He said I could stay in the room all day until it was time for the dinner show. He worked at Langley AFB. It all seemed like such a nice gesture.

When I arrived to Hampton, I went to my cousin's house. We carried on, reminiscing and telling funny stories. The next morning, I asked if my young son could stay at the house with her because I had some business to attend to and if it was okay, I would return the next morning for one more night's stay before returning to South Carolina.

I'd never been away from my son in another city and state, or any other place for that matter before. I left my son with her capable hands, and I arrived at 2 o'clock at the hotel and began resting. I never once called to check in on him. I was so focused on taking in a live show with a great friend of the family.

At the start of that evening, there was a rap on the door. It was Carrie. He wanted to come in to get dressed for the show. *Wait a minute, didn't you book your own room?* He explained there was a mix-up and after the show, it would be settled. One of us knew I was gullible and we both knew I was married. Someone in booking obviously made a huge mistake. Ain' nobody told me your husband's best friend isn't your best friend. This was one of those times when Daddy would say, "Think fast on your feet and don't take no wooden nickels." But I didn't get it until way further down the road.

After the show and dinner, which was absolutely grandeur, Carrie told me to go on up and he would take care of the rest. About four hours later, another rap came on the door from Carrie. He asked if he could bed down 'til morning. I thought to myself, "Why aren't you in your own room? Why don't you just drive home? You live only minutes away. Didn't you get the room saga fixed?" I suggested that I could just go back to my cousin's house, but he was not alright with that answer. He hinted that he could build a sheet barrier just for a few hours. He claimed he was tired and could not go another further. Without thinking, I said he could sleep on the couch.

I nestled down for the rest of my good sleep. I felt a touch and my body was quickened. With the absence of Burk's touch, Carrie's touch stirred me and woke up that hungry feeling.

Since I was in a different city and state, I allowed his bittersweet words to influence my thoughts. I went with it. From the words of his mouth, to the loneliness of my bed, to our bodies colliding, we were in a situation. However, the constant interruptions of calling out the name of my spouse, "Burk. Oh, Burk" while in a heap of passion, caused a major disruption in the flow of defiled pleasure. It was quite distasteful, but the only man I ever knew was Burk. With all the things done and said, being touched as a wife should be to her own husband. After a few times of those outbursts, it quenched and put out the fire for Carrie. I was embarrassed. I was sorry. I was left alone.

When I got back to my home in South Carolina, I found a letter in my bathroom window (for anyone to find) saying sorry for the corruptible things done to make me his and that he no longer wanted me to leave my husband. "Stay and work it out if you can," Carrie wrote.

Burk never admitted seeing the letter. I think he never did. Of course, I never asked. Carrie returned to Virginia, changed his contact information, and we never heard from him again.

THE DEATH OF GRIEF

No one knew, or at least I didn't know Burk was stuck in a world of grief and pain. He was dealing with his own struggles, problems, and demons while working on a job, trying to be a responsible adult. He would usually apologize to me and things would get better. Then things would get worse.

If I knew then what I know now, we probably never would have parted. Friends of my mama's church tried to sabotage my friendship with Burk. An old sister of the church, Nosey Dorothy, called my mama and told her that Burk had been married before with children. When she repeated to me what the sister said, I knew that would not be something to enter into. You don't marry a married man. How would that work? While in the background of Mama's stern conversations about the Bible and all the things I should NOT be doing, I was on the phone with him, letting him know I could not go with him because the secret was out that he was a married man, and there were children. He, of course, tried to convince me otherwise. While I was mad with the sister for meddling, she was an old Christian soldier, and we all believed her.

Burk told his mother and she called me to assure me that her son was NEVER married, and yes, he did have a child (a daughter named Beula), but she died at 18 months old. I felt absolutely saddened. His mother told me further that he was always talking about me. She felt that he really loved me and if it was any other way, she would say what the truth was.

After breaking off the relationship with Burk, I agreed to accept him back the very next day. He held in all the emotions of how his daughter died and all the events surrounding her death. He went to the Armed Forces and when he returned, all the drama of his own flesh and blood was before him. When his parents died, we were married. He never properly grieved. I saw how he dealt with pain.

He retreated, evaded, and medicated, but he would never talk. When I thought we could handle anything together, he shut me out. He fought me. The time was roughest when the epileptic seizures I suffered were happening more and more, and the birth of three sons, with our last son considered a little less than perfect. He went over the edge. I didn't understand his side. He couldn't understand my side. So much was going on. Death by grief scattered us and destroyed us. I made a decision to leave him so we all could remain and survive.

THE LOVE NO ONE SAW COMING

I was still married but separated for about 16 years. I asked GOD, "Does anyone see me?" All I was doing was what I was doing. I was taking care of my children, singing in church, playing the piano in church, and working an administration job IN CHURCH. Don't get me wrong, I absolutely loved church, the fellowship and camaraderie of the parishioners, the children, the work ethic, and the good pay. It was decent. It was demanding. I accepted a position in another city because where I was presently working, something totally outside my comfort zone happened to me.

Receiving love can be hard, especially if you were trying to receive it your whole life and it just wasn't reciprocated. People can share how much they think you're pretty, beautiful, talented, or classy, but you know they're lying because none of these conversations came to your ears and soul before. My music was mostly for my own benefit (to shield me, save me, heal me, and bless me). Others who listened were just a part of the moment in time and wrote themselves into my script.

I became the minister of music at the very fine Chapel Baptist Church in P-co. I was loved by the children, the seniors, the board of deacons, the pastor, and the choir. Five women from this ministry changed my life. We all sang together on the choir. These friends (my sisters in Christ) were tremendous and amazing to me. They helped me through a very volatile time in my life. One woman named Kelly took a more parental approach. She was the mother of the group. She worked for Social Services. She had a mother, son, and niece, and they all lived together. She had great taste in cars, clothes, and seemed to have great monetary means.

She took care of my children and me through a very physically challenging time. She helped me get a checking and a savings account. She also taught me and helped me with mutual funds and

Certificates of Deposit (CDs) for my children's future.

She taught me so much about life and I adored her for it. She had become my angel; my heroine. I was indebted to her. I wanted to make her as happy as she made me. Unknowingly, I gave her my power. She convinced me I could do nothing without her. I believed the acceptance of a woman who could sharpen me and touch me, who was smart and caring, was all I wanted from my own mama. Kelly supplied the fill for that discrepancy. It was the same as Mama, but it was different than Mama because I was accepted on a more personal and intimate level.

With the manic episodes, I sometimes would buy so many expensive things for the thrill and joy of having money. I would also have buyer's remorse, then hide my purchases from Kelly so she would not fuss. At those times, I would feel like a child. Ain' nobody told me I had the power to run my decisions.

Kelly helped me with practically everything, even the most personal details of my life. She helped me find the Adoptees & Birthparents In Search (Abis) Organization. From there, my whole birth family was found.

Sisterhood would have been a safe vehicle to ride in, but mania, and the other sicknesses penetrated the blurry lines. I believe I went from being needed to being needy. This vehicle was from a different place and time. I got lost. Lost in space. Lost in time. Lost from my own identity. Life was a conundrum. It was great, but daunting; and life was dreadful, but delightful.

I was invited to a Women's Tea Party by a friend from another ministry. This ministry was mostly a Caucasian congregation with a few brown people in the audience. The event was wonderful...until it got real. A woman was speaking prophetically in the room. I never saw her before and she didn't know me either. She started speaking some truths that could be a generic fit for anyone, but suddenly, she turned and started speaking to me directly. She spoke of things which only I knew. I knew GOD was talking to me and impressing upon me to get out while I could. Otherwise, I would die and it wouldn't go well.

When I had to leave Burk, one friend worked at the electric company and she got me set up with equal pay monthly for the bill. Another friend worked for the housing authority and she got me a nice brick house for a double-digit amount monthly. Another friend worked at the bank and she set me up with all my banking needs.

Me being the woman who wanted to die in times past, whose vital signs failed after being unconscious for several minutes, but was revived and couldn't believe that for the two times I tried to commit suicide in my youth, none of the attempts worked. I tried overdosing with some of the seizure medication and sedatives like Phenobarbital and Sinequan. I even used some scary big blue and grey capsules Mama took. They looked as if they were big enough to cause death in a young person, but they proved only to be Mama's blood pressure pills.

I wanted death because death seemed much better than what I was in. But I didn't want to die now or to die in a wrong place; a place where I could not come back from. I felt I had no choice but to leave the area and move away from my husband. My two older sons had moved west after high school to pursue college. I secretly rented a truck and took my youngest son and moved.

AIN' NOBODY TOLD ME I COULD STAND UP FOR MYSELF

So many people shared how they loved my writing, singing, and my humble attitude. I think a lot of my innate senses and talents were dominant in my genetics. My birth parents both sang. It wasn't until I found them that I knew where the singing and even my good looks came from. The teachings from my surrogate parents were necessary, though at times, they seemed very cruel. I believe they didn't get me as further along in my career because I played the 'humble' role, the 'I am unable to do this' role, and the 'I'm not good enough to do this' role. I was taught that.

In my upbringing, I was never made to feel that I would amount to anything, or that I was pretty or talented enough (when clearly, I was). I believed my mama against everyone else because she was my mama, and parents protect their children, right? I also believed she just didn't understand the full plight. Okay, being fair…no one knows the plight of their child. But with eyes wide open, you should be able to see what's going on and push them toward their dreams. My sons do that to their children. They support and they push. It's because they didn't have that as they were coming up. That's right! Their parents (Burk and I) failed them miserably in that. I was too afraid they would get hurt. My sons were able to break the curse.

This is my opinion. When in church, playing small came from pastors and teachers who wanted either for their own gain or some other reason have folk fit into the words from the Bible. "For I say, through the grace given unto me, to every man that is among you, not to think of himself more highly than he ought to think." Now this scripture is taken out of context for the most part, because the second half is usually never mentioned of the **Romans 12:3** scripture: "but to think soberly, according as God hath dealt to every man the measure of faith."

One should not be arrogant, but one can be self-assured and confident. These are not evil terms. God gave us all what we have, and faith causes us to go after what we know we have. I have ears. I can hear me. I can even feel me. Yes, I know I can sing. I have imagination and memory with a sense of language style. I know I can write. However, fear kept me out of the real doors. Believing the hype of 'you're gonna make it,' but not sowing into my own gift, thinking someone else is supposed to make me famous, was a major loss. All of these were false hopes. It was NEVER in faith because I never went outside my comfort zone to test or activate FAITH to the level of what I really desired! Reminiscent of the classic movie "On the Waterfront" when Marlon Brando said, "I cudda been a contender, I cudda been somebody," these were my regretful moans and groans. I cry at every motivational speech I hear or when seeing someone young trying toward their dreams. I've seen some people turned around, but they were strong enough to get to their YONDER PLACE, and were strong enough to do it again, again, and again.

I was feeling confident in my youth when I sent my music to Andraé Crouch and to Light and Word Records founder Ralph Carmichael. I was rejected right off the bat. That put me on an extended pause. But in my young adult years, on a local level, I entered and won talent shows. I sang at weddings, for the governor, and with many artists, such as Donnie Harper & the New Jersey Mass Choir, John P. Kee, Richard Smallwood, Helen Baylor, Babbie Mason, and the Gaithers. My music was accepted at James Cleveland's Gospel Music Workshop of America (GMWA) and I sang at the annual convention's New Artist Showcase. Those were amazing times.

In the early 2000s, I was in my own bed sleeping when a man named Mr. Smythe called looking for me. He explained that a gentleman coerced him to call my number because of my induction to my state's

Arts Commission. When he came over, he auditioned on his trumpet. He was amazing, so I auditioned for him. That too was amazing. We spent time from that Thursday evening cultivating a relationship. Two years later, we were wed. It was my 'wuz-band'[9] Burk who introduced us. Go figure!

Mr. Smythe and I made music together and traveled the United States doing my written songs in my mid-life years. I even won a competition for Dorinda Clark Cole and auditioned for Sunday's Best. Yes, I've had many opportunities. One would say, "You did it!" or "You've arrived!" I tried, but there is more to do. I know I'm supposed to be in music. I know I'm to be a life-changing writer. It's like the breath I am now breathing. In my seasoned years, I don't think I've lost the courage, just some of the stamina. So many things have happened. It was one thing after the other. A head-on crash by a drunk, two broken femurs, mania, panic attacks, diabetes, two TIA, and then a larger brain injury (a stroke) that left me debilitated on the left side, extensive therapies to include trapezius muscle sprain, femur break and surgery, stroke rehabilitation, son knocked into a coma, and same son had pneumonia three different times.

There was one thing I learned in therapy: Consistency is the key. It's the same in your dreams, visions, goals, and in business. If it doesn't come to you, you go to it and make it happen.

---

[9] Former husband: "was"

FROM DEMOTION TO PROMOTION

I had an invitation to sing at the Pink Elephant, a club for young adult Christians. It was rather chic. They served cute little named food like Heaven's Wings, Angel Eggs, Eden's Garden Salad, etc. There was a house band and they were the epitome of polished musicians. I happened to be called on Jazz night. I'd never sang in a club before, so I didn't know how things were ran. For as much as they would let me, I used my chops that night. People appeared to like the vibe. I sang and sang and sang. But ain' nobody told me there were other people up to sing. Although they talked to me during the set and exchanged a few numbers, I never got called to perform there again.

However, from that gig, I was contacted to sing at a ministry in the city. It was a different type of revival. It was a prayer seminar. I was asked to do an A and B selection. When I got there, I hurried up to get inside because the music sounded so amazing. It was just like some evangelical shows on TV. Lots of space and cameras galore. Quite frankly, although I felt as if I were in a Hollywood church, I also got the sense I had come home.

I was called to sing, so shaking like a leaf, I went to the piano, greeted the people, and sung my version of the Folgers Coffee song. The jingle was familiar, so they laughed at a certain time in the song. I canvased the sanctuary, saw on the front row was a couple from Camelot looking quite regal, and I was in their kingdom. It was a tight-knit community. You could just tell. The pastor was extremely handsome with a million-dollar smile that complimented his deeply rich dark complexion. His wife was no less in beauty. She, as well as he, was well dressed and manicured.

The pastor gave over the sacred desk a compliment to me of my style, my voice, my anointing. He liked me. I think the others did too. Some time had passed and his deep dark voice was on the other end of the phone one afternoon asking if I could play for a weekday funeral. I wasn't in demand that day, so I agreed. I drove west and played. After the service, he came over to me and said, "That was tremendous. That was absolutely tremendous." I smiled with a sigh of relief because I never played for any church like that before and I was as nervous as could be.

Another span of time went by and the pastor of that esteemed church called. This time, he called to let me know he was in the market for a minstrel. I was certainly interested, but felt inadequate based on the musicianship of his former keyboardist. He played like GOD. I loved his singing and keyboard style.

The pastor set up a meeting for us at 2:30 p.m. It went absolutely horrible. First off, I was late. He was short on patience and quite rude. He yelled at me as if I were his four-year-old. His debonair way brought me to pause. He asked if I liked the ministry and if I would like to play for the worship services. He said he would give me a weekly job and a couple of allowances to supplement my pay. I would get $325 a week, plus a gas allowance and a housing allowance, which equated to almost $370. I was really cool with that. He rattled off the job description, gave the do's and don'ts, and asked would I be alright with it all.

Of course, I said, "Yes." But I let him know I don't play like Sean, his former musician. He came at me with the harshness and aggression of a foot going for a water bug.

"Did I ask you to play like Sean? I didn't ask you to play like Sean! Either you want the job or you don't. I'm not paying more than that. And have me a great music program." With little less passion, he said, "I know you can do it. I really love your spirit. The Holy Ghost and you are one."

While in his ranting, I thought, "Hmm, somebody's on his period." After he brought his voice to a calm, I was able to come in the same tone to say I would accept the position. At that time, I was still living in eastern South Carolina. I commuted for about five months back and forth. During the sudden illness of my youngest son, I tried to keep up the pace, so I made the decision to move to the metro area. I was in work/church heaven. My nine-year tenure to this Gospel church was absolutely amazing. However, somewhere in the middle of my dedication to the ministry, I started seeing things without my rose-colored glasses on. There were many instances where I challenged the system because I am naturally inquisitive.

Every year, I had to have an evaluation to see if my medication changes were working and to see if I showed any improvement in order to continuing receiving disability payments from Supplemental Security Income (SSI) due to epilepsy and vascular migraines. (I never had a secular job because music always paid my bills.) An evaluation date had been set and I was sent postal mail from SSI. The letters were mailed three months prior to the appointment so everyone's schedules may comply. I took a copy of my letter to work one day in May for Boss Lady, as I affectionately called her, to see and add to my file. I saw her write it on her calendar and put the copy in the cabinet of my file folder. Three months later, August 12th, I got up that Tuesday morning to ready myself for the evaluation. I went to the mental eval first, then the medical testing. The appointment could last as long as six hours between testing and going to the doctor.

On this day, my appointment wasn't as long as it was supposed to be, so I stopped by the church office to see everyone, share my experience, and do a little something if I needed to. As I was pulling into the parking lot, Boss Lady was leaving. When she saw my car, she turned around. As I was gearing up to get out, she had parked and gotten out of her vehicle to walk inside the building. I, unaware of her contempt, spoke to her in my usual chipper manner. She did not reciprocate, but responded with retaliation.

"Miss Juanita, meet me in my office now!"

I remember asking her, "Who licked the red off your candy?"

She replied, "You!"

I thought nothing of her response because I know how sometimes she was in deep thought. Maybe she didn't even understand my question. She had her power walk on and she seemed to be focused. Maybe she just wrote a song. She liked writing and sometimes she'd ask me to set music to some of her songs for the praise team to sing. Upon entering the building, I turned a hard left to go to my office to grab a notepad and pen. When I got to her office, she was already at her desk, reclined in her chair, with her boots on her desk.

"Close the door."

"Yes, ma'am."

"You know I fire people who do not come to work."

"Ma'am?"

I was completely caught off guard by her statement. I reminded her that today was the 12th, and I had a standing SSI Evaluation appointment starting at 9 a.m.

"Don't you remember? I brought you a copy of my appointment and you wrote it on your calendar, plus you put it in my file," I said.

"I didn't hear from you, you didn't call in, you just missed a whole day of work. I fire people who do not show up for work!"

Of course, I was not worried because none of this applied to me. She was well notified. Then the most unimaginable thing happened.

"Miss Jaimas, go to your office and pack it up and clear it out. You're fired!"

I could tell she was trying to pull my chain. She wanted me to react to what she said, but she didn't know that Maree was my mama, and I've learned how NOT to react to authority. I just looked at her with my tempered body language, submissive eyes, no reaction, and said, "Okay."

She went in the back to get a cart for me to carry my things out to the car. I made about four trips before the computer question. I was dating Mr. Smythe (trumpeter and Information Technology geek) then and he gave me the computer for my office. As I was gathering my things, I went to ask Boss Lady if I should leave the computer or take it with me.

"Is it mine?"

"No, ma'am. Mr. Smythe gave it to me for the office."

"Well, no. It's yours. Take it. I don't want it."

This was when I realized she was contemptuous and wanted me out and gone. Her next words were even more baffling than the former words.

"And you'd BETTER be in church Wednesday night for Bible Study!"

I was about to take the computer outfit; the last thing from my office to my car. She was poised at the door, with her legs crossed like the number four. She watched me put the last things in the car and push her cart back to the building. When I was about to say goodbye, she looked me square in the eyes and said, "Now when you return to work in the morning at 9:00 sharp, I want you to remember this moment. For if you ever pull a stunt like you pulled today, you will be fired for real. I do expect you to attend all church and business

91

functions for this ministry. Understood?"

The other workers had their doors open, listening to the tomfoolery going on in the hall. I simply said, "I will be here at 10 because I have to wait for my son to board the bus."

I just walked out. *What was that?* I felt mocked, humiliated, and disrespected. I believe she knew she went too far. I sat in my car for several moments, trying to make sense of what just happened. I was too embarrassed to tell my sons or my beau. I called my church daughter and told her what happened. She said, "Mama, I told you she doesn't like you."

I defended her by saying, "Maybe she had a bad day. She loves me though."

"Okay, 'Miss she loves me.' Are you going to report her for doing that to you? You should, Mama."

I said to my play daughter, "She couldn't fire me because she didn't hire me. She just did that because her husband is in Africa."

I drove home under a cloud, wondering why she got so much pleasure out of demeaning me.

I suffered many vicious and petty acts from the heads of this ministry. In fact, I have stories for days about the cynical treatment I received. I was there to serve them, but I know God called me to serve any place, anywhere, anytime. Position and Placement doesn't really matter to me. I can serve anywhere, and in any capacity, but posture is what's most important to me. My heart's motive and willingness must be pure to God first.

Eventually, one Wednesday night, I did turn in my resignation letter with my husband by my side. On Sunday morning after I played the entire service, the pastor called me in his office to scold me about the resignation, then he fired me.

They did hurt me, but I was in it for the long haul. I was in it because GOD called me. When he thought I would be broken by getting fired, I got encouraged and God gave me a spiritual promotion!

THE HATE NO ONE SAW COMING

Looking back over my lifespan, I discovered I am a creature of habit. We all are creatures of change and reinvention. We steadily try on this and remove that, trying to reinvent ourselves as great, good, or indifferent. We change our eye color, hair color, bleach our skin, get eyelash extensions, hair wigs and weaves, false fingernails and toenails, shrink in weight or get buffed up, or get in debt to make ourselves seem good or we do it to make someone else feel bad. Whatever the case, we're on the side of happy and confident, or unfulfilled and unattractive.

Oddly enough though, the more we change, the more we remain the same. You are the baby your mama once delivered. You are you, but you are not that baby anymore. Evolution takes place and we grow, advance, and progress. Spirit and soul must agree. However, in all of this, some things never change.

Baffled beyond my means to articulate or comprehend was the Wednesday evening my oldest sister called me. It was June 17, 2015. I got the call around ten o'clock in the evening. I was editing some papers for a friend.

"Nita, our nephew, Tywanza and Aunt Suzie dead."

"What?"

I'm thinking they were headed to Walmart and got struck by a car in Ty's car. It's one of those quiet days of the week, so how could this happen? As I tried to rationalize in my thoughts an accident that takes two of our family members instantly, I asked Sustah, "So was it a car crash?"

She answered back, "No! Deh get kill in church! Go cut on deh

TV."

I ran to the television, turned to CNN, and there it was, the story I could not begin to fathom. As the story was unfolding, I was fixed at the edge of my comforting recliner, hoping for the anchor to say it was *fake news*, so the report would come to an end. I clicked to the local news stations also. They were all saying the same thing. Night and day, I kept looking in shock and horror, waiting for words like *hoax, practical joke,* or *prank,* but those words would never be heard because those words could never be said. It was true. It was all surreal, but true. I sat in one spot for three days. My husband supported me by sitting with me, crying with me, and praying with me. I was unable to speak to anyone for months. All I could do was cry. I thought back to the four little girls bombed in their church in September 15, 1963, in Birmingham, Alabama. The most hallowed of grounds, the most sacred haven…destroyed.

My darling husband offered to drive me to Johns Island to see Sustah. When we got there, there were many, many supporters. Sustah greeted my husband, K, and me at the door. She said she had cooked a few things that were in the oven and there were other dishes and drinks people brought. She beckoned me to get something to eat. I couldn't get over the fact she was up, talking, and rehearsing the events of that fateful massacre only a few nights ago. Sustah's husband was quiet in a corner with a continuous flow of tears, while she had a continuous flow of conversation.

I asked, "Sustah, shouldn't you be upstairs on Valium?" She gave me a big squeeze and a kiss. "The Lord's got it all in control."

Yes, we're Christians, but I did not want to hear that God is a God of justice and a God of judgment. Where is the justice? Where is the judgment?

I was sore angry. This event changed me in a way I could not rationalize. It almost changed the theology of my Christendom. All I did was cry. I cried daily for two years, sobbing uncontrollably. I was a solopreneur, with my company just getting off the ground for the third year. I was broken, suspended, and stopped.

I wanted to go to the Narrow River, take a ladder to the bottom, take a seat at the river's floor, and give way to my soul, my spirit, and my mind. My body would have to follow.

How could this Caucasian child, slightly older than a teen, have these diabolical thoughts about life and black people? He said we were responsible for the raping of "their" women, we're trying to take over, and he just could not allow that to happen, so he had to do something. He said several times that he was not sorry for what he did. He spoke for himself because he didn't want to be looked at as insane or mentally ill. Wow! The evil act he committed already placed him in that category.

His history was sorely blurred. But hey, we were always told white lies about ourselves. We're ignorant, goons, coons, jigaboos, monkeys, and not even a person. When in fact, the bitter truth is, we are the superior race with dignity, poise, culture, smarts, creativity, ethics, morals, and the list goes on and on.

Out of all that was formulated to bring a deliberate race war, nevertheless, it was turned and backfired right back in his face. Dylann Roof did not succeed. Even though the driving force for this massacre was HATE, LOVE FROM A PEOPLE OF A RICH CULTURE IN GOD PREVAILED!

Sustah was the fourth person to speak to the judge on the 17th at the bond hearing. The emotion was unanimous. FORGIVENESS. Sustah said to him, "We welcomed you Wednesday night in our Bible Study with open arms. You have killed some of the most beautifulest people that I know. Every fiber in my body hurts." She continued saying her son was her hero and concluded by saying the full consensus of the room. "We forgive you, but may God have mercy on you. I forgive you."

Boy! What does one do with that? Every day for the rest of his natural life, Dylann will wake up in hell. From a place of self-loathing and hatred of brown-skinned people (of whom he had friends who were), to him hearing, seeing, and feeling FORGIVENESS.

It's got to be awful to receive what you don't want. Forgiveness. It sort of reminds me of the story about the two thieves. One was a smart aleck. They were all set to die, but his smart mouth and his cynical heart wounded up in a separate place than the other thief and Jesus.

The only thing these two people lacked, Roof and the thief, was belief. To believe in something larger than yourself is promising. It takes the pressure off you and places it on the higher power.

The day of the sentencing was indescribable. I was teeter tottering between sad and mad, hurt and numbness. When Roof was given the death penalty, it didn't make me feel any better. I felt like a criminal for wanting him to get the 'payback.' I learned something about myself during this event of life, death, freedom, love, hate, justice, and judgment. We are all at the mercy of them all.

The tangerine truths are not shocking to us. We already knew in our royal persona that we are special. This is why we were made to be broken, sacrificed, killed, and destroyed.

Everyone alive is capable of loving and love, hatred and killing, hope and believing, trusting and faith.

You may have heard this saying, "Faith comes by hearing…,"[10] but

---

[10] **Romans 10:17**

doubt comes the very same way. You take on what you hear, see, and experience.

We all have evil in us, and we all have good in us. No matter how cute, quiet, talented, smart, or whatever, we all are capable of the worst thing and the best thing. Everyone must choose their own path and how to live out their days. Reinvention will constantly be on the stage.

AIN' NOBODY EVER TOLD YOU?

Ain' nobody ever told you, you was special?

Ain' dat the devil?

I think you clever wit'cho crazy self,

Always talking dat faith talk,

Putting your cares on dah shelf and some you put high up in the sky,

Tell dat devil he's a lie.

Ain' gon steal my joy,

I got somewhere to go,

I know the devil's ploy.

Ain' nobody ever told you, you was perty?

Always wearing your uniform for the streets and the church,

Well, I ain' never seen you dirty.

Ain' got no dollars, but you got plenty sense.

Always talking dat Jesus talk.

Well, at least every time I see yah,

Your faith be deep and wide.

You say sump'in like dis,

"I'm just crazy enough to believe,"

'Cuz all things are possible when you get up off your knees.

I ain' never heard compliments from where it matters,

Serving up ridicules on big white platters,

It got in my head, with mirrors and glasses shattered.

But I learned the truth.

I should build up my own self,

Take myself down from dying on the shelf.

Listen,

I ain' never heard I was special.

But I am, and you are too;

Or that I was perty,

But I am, and you are too;

Or even that I had sense,

But I do, and you do too.

We is all rich 'cuz somebody done turn on the prosperity switch.

'Cuz blessings are flowing from the windows of heaven,

But ain' no need to get puffed up like leaven.

The Lord giveth and the Lord taketh away,

Blessed be the name of the Lord,

Keep your head together, I say!

Ain' nobody ever told you, you did something right?

Don't do nothing for another's applause.

'Cuz you might be waiting forever to hear clever words gone bad.

Do what you do for your own satisfaction,

Knowing that GOD gave you His power to accomplish His actions.

We're all the same even as we are all different deep down within.

You have nothing together,

But you have it all together with GOD.

That should be no riddle…

God is the author with His beginning, and endings,

And we make the stories in the middle.

LESSONS FROM THE KING

When I look at my son, K, I see the epitome of success. K could care less who says what about him. He believes his own press. He loved the TV show *Life Goes On* with the actor Chris Burke.[11] He then got his hopes on being an actor. Although K cannot write or read very well, he'd say, "One day, I'm going to be a weatherman and an actor." So, every season he pretended he was in this fine drama, with a starring role or a supporting role as an actor. He has a great imagination. But in real-life, he was featured on the local news with the meteorologist doing the weather. That was so awesome.

When I think of K, I think of no fear, no inhibitions. On the golf course, he is *Tiger Weed*, on the basketball court, he is *Michael Gordon*, and in Karate, he is *Fruse-lee!* He is a man of few words and a simple lifestyle. He ONLY does think that brings him closer to his goals. He only watches wrestling on TV, unless he's repeating one of the movies he owns on dogs and cowboy shows. He has a library of periodicals and magazines. He's only focuses on his own dreams.

He became the president and CEO of his company. K has always been my most studious child. He was actually the first owner of a business, the K CAN ENTERPRISE. He loves books, paper, and being in charge.

He left that profession to become KING. He remains King. When he's not in lordship, he is sheriff or a K9 policeman. He is always in the state of becoming. He has continuous courage to speak those things that are not, as though they were.[12]

He sees himself as a man of means with great authority. I dare not

---

[11] First actor with Down Syndrome to be in a TV network series
[12] **Romans 4:17**

squash his dreams or his imagination. But it doesn't even matter. He doesn't let anybody come against who he is or is becoming.

When life gets really hard and some mean-spirited people bully him, he graces his imagination with thoughts of his next birthday and the spectacular time he will have with family and friends.

When K was released from the hospital from a serious car crash, he was released with a tracheostomy (trach) tube. After the trach was in for a while, he wanted to have a solo concert with all his favorite songs. He was motivating himself to keep going. I prepared the video camera, dressed him for his debut concert, and he sang about five songs at the pinnacle of his lungs. He loves to sing. He sings his songs to GOD, and heaven loves it. It's a bit difficult to sing beside him, but he would never be heard saying, "I can't sing." He sang his heart out for God that day.

Challenging circumstances should never dictate or override what you want to accomplish or who you want to be. Yes, he was born with Down's Syndrome. They said he would be late in most developmental things and they said he wouldn't live. He has superseded all of the naysayers. He has great success!

What a lesson from such a wonderful dreamer. What a wonderful spirit. What wonderful tenacity. Go get 'em, big dawg!

EPILOGUE

There are countless events in our lives where we can get lost because we lose our focus, ourselves, love, God, and straight tenacity. When someone vows to love you, you expect that hurt won't come along with the package, unless there is a true antidote to heal. No matter how you try, you will eventually hurt the person you love. Family, friendships, marriage, and children are tied into the heart/emotions.

When people's expectancy gets too high, or part of the relationship is compromised, taking each other for granted or making assumptions can become volatile attributes. However, when respect, communication, and the GOD FACTOR come into play, there is a winning outcome. Everyone born in this world has a plight, a journey to make, a destiny to pursue. YOU are the only one able to do your journey and write your story. Everyone's story is similar, yet distinctively different.

I came in the world as a low-weight premature baby with a mountain of issues, rejection, health challenges, surrogate parents (perhaps above the age limit for childrearing), and social and mental challenges. Yet I was given a gift to communicate through a smile, being happy, having a giving heart, being joyful, singing, playing a musical instrument, and writing stories and songs.

I realized ten important lessons in life:

- Ain' nobody told my mama about abuse, what abuse was, or how to treat someone less powerful than you...no one told me either. I learned what she didn't know and made it my truth and reality, while adding some *'make my own sense of things'* element to this life doctrine of *parenthood, spouse, friend, and self.*

- My grandmother was the first teacher when she said, "Love! Love, child, 'til you can't love no mo. Love 'til love come spilling from your veins and out your ears. BUT...Save some love for yourself!" This is PIVOTAL! God says, "Love ME first, then love yourself, and then other people."[13]

The next few lessons came from my daddy:

- Don't let nobody talk you out of what you can do or what you can be.

- You might give out, but don't give up. Your foot is on the gas to drive it anywhere you can, and you'll know how fast to go.

- You work the job. Don't let the job work you!

- Learn to live with a thing, not in it!

- There is never a second education in the first kick of a mule!

- Preparation time is never lost time. (Dr. Leon Threatt)

- Excuses are the crutches of the uncommitted. (A.R. Bernard)

- Swear to your own hurt and change not! (**Psalm 15:4**)

Daddy had only a second grade education, but he was lavished with wisdom. Every word from his lips was a lesson; a nugget to live by.

Maturity ultimately found its place in my world. I didn't give up on me, and a heck of a lot more people didn't give up on me either. I have reared my children to the best of my ability. The things I did to my children were a result of what I was taught through my parents' parenting style.

---

[13] **Mark 12:30-31**

Initially, before I became a parent, I said I would never beat my children. I would love them into doing right. But my vow waned as different situations arose in my inquisitive and testing children. Ain' nobody told us about abuse. When the white man had us enslaved and oppressed, ain' nobody said that was abuse.

I do believe that when you become a parent, you automatically know a lot of things. It is innate. However, there are lots more we have to experience and learn.

My parents, who were old, were doing the best they could with what they had. I was essentially a child trying to train children with not a lot of knowledge on how. So let me be clear. It's not about age!

There were practices and disciplines my mother used that I never used when raising my own children. Did I make mistakes? You doggone skippy I did. I made huge mistakes, but grace gave me multiple chances. My boys loved me. They hated me. But regardless of feelings, I couldn't shut them out. I had to let them express themselves, regardless of the hurt I might have felt. Whatever they were feeling was important enough to listen to and learn the lessons that helped to push us further in our parent-adult-child relationship.

With the help of the LORD, now I have a clearer outlook on love, relationships, and life. A famous quote says, "Wisdom is the principal thing; therefore get wisdom: and with all thy getting get understanding."[14] Every day is a new beginning to rehearse what was learned. My grandchildren and great-grands will be the beneficiaries of a legacy of healthy loving…with no trauma.

I'm so glad I wasn't aborted or that I didn't abort my own self. I have daily opportunities to write, sing, be a wife, mama, grandmama,

---

[14] **Proverbs 4:7**

friend, a whole woman, a businesswoman, a moral woman, and a woman who is always fertile with ideas, goals, and imagination! I am successful because I have love, family, God, and the nature and instinct to go get what is needed for each phase.

Know your worth. Say what God is saying. Don't take "NO" for the final answer, because all you need is one YES!

You can change the direction of your life. I was called unsuccessful all my life, but I saw something different, so I did something different.

Once you know better, you will do better, and then pay it forward for someone else to do better too.

Learn what abuse is and what it looks like on you, to you, and with you!

Finally, DON'T YOU SETTLE for the worst. You are the best!